W9-AAV-034

ANGKOR WAT
& SIEM REAP

ENCOUNTER

NICK RAY

Angkor Wat & Siem Reap Encounter

Published by Lonely Planet Publications Pty Ltd
ABN 36 005 607 983

Australia	Head Office, Locked Bag 1, Footscray, Vic 3011
	☎ 03 8379 8000 fax 03 8379 8111
	talk2us@lonelyplanet.com.au
USA	150 Linden St, Oakland, CA 94607
	☎ 510 250 6400
	toll free 800 275 8555
	fax 510 893 8572
	info@lonelyplanet.com
UK	2nd fl, 186 City Rd
	London EC1V 2NT
	☎ 020 7106 2100 fax 020 7106 2101
	go@lonelyplanet.co.uk

This title was commissioned in Lonely Planet's Melbourne office and produced by: **Commissioning Editors** Suzannah Shwer, Carolyn Boicos **Coordinating Editors** Stephanie Pearson, Dianne Schallmeiner **Cartographers** Erin McManus, Peter Shields **Layout Designer** Indra Kilfoyle **Senior Editor** Katie Lynch **Managing Cartographer** David Connolly **Cover Designer** Pepi Bluck **Project Manager** Rachel Imeson **Series Designer** Mik Ruff **Thanks to** Helen Christinis, Jennifer Garrett, Geoff Howard

Cover photograph Buddhist monks crossing lake at Angkor, Hugh Sitton/Corbis **Internal photographs** p31, p51, p63, p81, p95 by Nick Ray. All other photographs by Lonely Planet Images, and by Felix Hug except p60 John Banagan; p76 Anders Blomqvist; p113 Daniel Boag; p110 Frank Carter; p46 Sara-Jane Cleland; p26-7, p55 Juliet Coombe; p93 Richard I'Anson

All images are copyright of the photographers unless otherwise indicated. Many of the images in this guide are available for licensing from **Lonely Planet Images:** www.lonelyplanetimages.com.

ISBN 978 1 74179 426 7

Printed through Colorcraft Ltd, Hong Kong.
Printed in China.

HOW TO USE THIS BOOK
Colour-Coding & Maps

Colour-coding is used for symbols on maps and in the text that they relate to (eg all eating venues on the maps and in the text are given a green knife and fork symbol). Each region also gets its own colour, and this is used down the edge of the page and throughout that region section.

Send us your feedback We love to hear from readers — your comments help make our books better. We read every word you send us, and we always guarantee that your feedback goes straight to the appropriate authors. The most useful submissions are rewarded with a free book. To send us your updates and find out about Lonely Planet events, newsletters and travel news visit our award-winning website: **www.lonelyplanet.com/contact**.

Note: We may edit, reproduce and incorporate your comments in Lonely Planet products such as guidebooks, websites and digital products, so let us know if you don't want your comments reproduced or your name acknowledged. For a copy of our privacy policy visit **www.lonelyplanet.com/privacy**.

NICK RAY

Nick first glimpsed Angkor in a dusty old encyclopaedia and knew he had to go. He finally visited in 1995, marking the start of an enduring love affair that has seen him settle in Cambodia and work around the temples in a number of roles, from Lonely Planet cycling-guide author to location manager on *Lara Croft: Tomb Raider*. Nick lives in Phnom Penh, and makes regular forays up to Angkor for guidebooks, articles, tours and TV work. He also enjoys Siem Reap and has witnessed its transition from a sleepy village to a tourist magnet. The wining and dining scene has definitely improved with age. Nick has written for several guidebooks on Cambodia, including Lonely Planet's *Cambodia* and *Southeast Asia on a Shoestring*.

NICK'S THANKS

A huge, heartfelt thanks to the people of Siem Reap, who have always provided a warm welcome. Biggest thanks to my wife Kulikar Sotho and our young son Julian for encouraging the adventures and joining me on some. Thanks to fellow travellers, residents, friends and contacts in Cambodia who have helped shaped my knowledge and experience. You know who you are. Finally, thanks to the Lonely Planet in-house team who have steered this edition to fruition.

THE PHOTOGRAPHER

Felix Hug used to shoot hoops for a professional basketball team in Switzerland before he decided that shooting images was more enjoyable. In 2007, Felix was the runner-up at the Travel Photographer of the Year awards. He received an honourable mention at the PDN/National Geographic Traveler 'World in Focus' contest in 2005 and took home the Asian Geographic Nikon Grand Prize in 2004. Felix believes that the job of the travel photographer is to capture inspiring images instead of just documenting reality: 'Positive images and compassion will inspire and change the way we look at things.'

Our readers Many thanks to the travellers who wrote to us with helpful hints, useful advice and interesting anecdotes: Bianca Barbaro, Kathy Belpaeme, Jason Brown, Pablo Contestabile, Bryan Cronk, Brent Kendall, Tracey Seslen, Melanie Simunovic, Mark Westerfield.

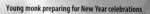
Young monk preparing for New Year celebrations

CONTENTS

Our authors are independent, dedicated travellers. They don't research using just the internet or phone, and they don't take freebies, so you can rely on their advice being well researched and impartial. They travel widely visiting thousands of places, taking great pride in getting all the details right and telling it how it is.

THIS IS ANGKOR WAT & SIEM REAP

There is no greater concentration of architectural riches anywhere on earth. Choose from the world's largest religious building, Angkor Wat; one of the world's weirdest, Bayon; or the riotous jungle of Ta Prohm.

Beyond the big three are dozens more temples, each of which would be the star were it located anywhere else in the region. Take Banteay Srei, the art gallery of Angkor; Preah Khan, the ultimate fusion temple; or Beng Mealea, the *Titanic* of temples, suffocating under the jungle. The most vexing part of a visit to Angkor is working out what to see, as there are simply so many spectacular sites.

Abandoned to the jungle for centuries, the magnificent temples are set amid the region's oldest national park, with towering trees and a refreshing lack of development. It is possible to plan a peaceful pilgrimage here, far from the madding crowds.

Life continues amid the temples. Visit the villages around Angkor to experience the timeless landscapes of rice paddies and swaying sugar palms. Or cruise through the floating villages of Tonlé Sap lake, an incredible world on water.

The temples grab the headlines and deservedly so, but Siem Reap is no slouch as the gateway to ancient treasures. Wiped from the map by war and genocide, Cambodia is the comeback kid of Southeast Asia, and nowhere is this more tangible than in Siem Reap. Few towns on earth are expanding this fast, as Siem Reap sucks in those seeking to take advantage of its newfound status as Asia's historic hot spot.

Despite the headlining act that is Angkor and the contemporary chic of Siem Reap, Cambodia's greatest treasure is its people. The Khmers have been to hell and back, but they have prevailed with a smile; no visitor comes away from this enigmatic kingdom without a measure of admiration and affection for its inhabitants.

Top left The sun goes down over Angkor Wat (p60) **Bottom left** Thirsty work on Tonlé Sap lake (p16)

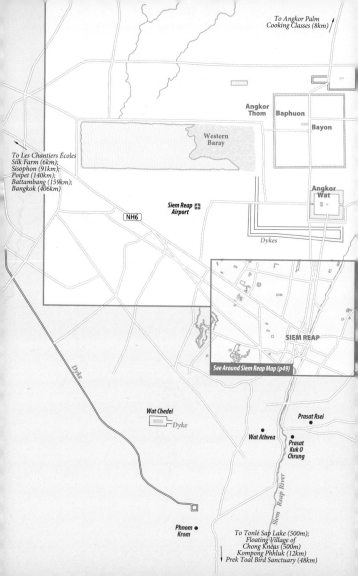

To Angkor Palm
Cooking Classes (8km)

Angkor
Thom   **Baphuon**

Bayon

Western
Baray

To Les Chantiers Écoles
Silk Farm (6km);
Sisophon (91km);
Poipet (140km);
Battambang (159km);
Bangkok (406km);

Angkor
Wat

Siem Reap
Airport

NH6

Dykes

SIEM REAP

See Around Siem Reap Map (p49)

Dyke

Wat Chedei
Dyke

Prasat Rsei

Wat Athvea   *Prasat*
Kuk O
Chrung

Siem Reap River

Phnom
Krom

To Tonlé Sap Lake (500m);
Floating Village of
Chong Kneas (500m)
Kompong Phhluk (12km)
Prek Toal Bird Sanctuary (48km)

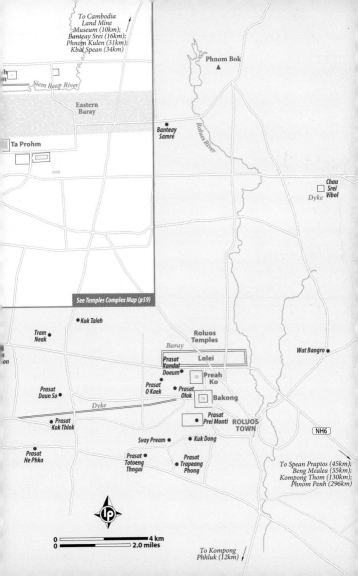

To Cambodia
Land Mine
Museum (10km);
Banteay Srei (16km);
Phnom Kulen (31km);
Kbal Spean (34km)

Phnom Bok ▲

Siem Reap River

Eastern
Baray

Banteay
Samré

Rolous River

Ta Prohm

Chau
Srei
Vibol

Dyke

See Temples Complex Map (p59)

Kuk Taleh

Tram
Neak

Roluos
Temples

Baray

Wat Bangro

Prasat
Kandal
Doeum

Lolei

Prasat
O Kaek

Preah
Ko

Prasat
Olak

Prasat
Daun So

Dyke

Bakong

Prasat
Kok Thlok

Prasat
Prei Monti

ROLUOS
TOWN

Prasat
He Phka

Svay Pream

Kuk Dong

NH6

Prasat
Totoeng
Thngai

Prasat
Trapeang
Phong

To Spean Praptos (45km);
Beng Mealea (55km);
Kompong Thom (130km);
Phnom Penh (296km)

0   4 km
0   2.0 miles

LP

To Kompong
Phhluk (12km)

>HIGHLIGHTS

The overgrown beauty of Ta Phrom (p79)

>1 ANGKOR WAT

WITNESS SUNRISE OVER THE HOLIEST OF THE HOLIES

The traveller's first glimpse of Angkor Wat, the ultimate expression of Khmer genius, is simply staggering and is matched by only a few select spots on earth, such as Machu Picchu and Petra.

Soaring skyward and surrounded by a moat that would make its European castle counterparts blush, Angkor Wat is one of the most inspired and spectacular monuments ever conceived by the human mind. It is a sumptuous blend of form and function, a spellbinding shrine to Vishnu and, with its captivating image replicated in the reflective pools below, a feast for unbelieving eyes.

Angkor Wat is the most popular spot for sunrise around Angkor, and not without good reason. The sun shifts position depending on the time of year, and during the equinoxes of March (20/21) and September (22/23) it rises directly over the central tower of Angkor Wat. Sometimes it's a glowing ball of orange emerging above the cloud line; at other times flaming streaks of cirrus clouds paint the sky blood-red, providing a dramatic backdrop to the temple. But even if it doesn't deliver, don't be disappointed – this is always a magical and mesmerising place to be at dawn.

Dawn comes early to Angkor and modern-day pilgrims need to leave their abodes before 5.30am to experience sunrise over the fabled temple. Enter from the west with the majority and stake a quiet spot near one of the libraries, or enter in solitude from the east, creeping through the forest and see the light slowly reveal Angkor Wat's iconic towers. As the tour groups flood back to town for breakfast, stick around and explore this wondrous sight without the crowds.

Plans are afoot to light Angkor Wat by night to ease crowd congestion, which could make an atmospheric alternative to sunrise.

See p60 for more information.

ANGKOR WAT: HEART & SOUL OF A NATION

Angkor is everywhere: it's on the flag, it's the national beer, it's hotels and guest-houses, it's even cigarettes. It's a symbol of nationhood, of fierce pride, a fingers-up to the world that says no matter how bad things have become, you can't forget the fact that we, the Cambodians, built Angkor Wat. Even the destructive Khmer Rouge paid homage to the mighty Angkor Wat on their flag. This helps explain why the Khmers get so mad with the neighbouring Thais for claiming Angkor Wat as their temple, a misrepresentation of history that is still taught in Thai schools.

>2 ANGKOR THOM

EXPLORE THE EXPRESSIVE MONUMENTS OF THE 'GREAT CITY'

It's hard to imagine any building bigger or more beautiful than Angkor Wat, but in Angkor Thom the sum of the parts add up to a greater whole. The gates grab you first, flanked by a monumental representation of the Churning of the Ocean of Milk: 54 demons and 54 gods engaged in an epic tug-of-war. Each gate towers above the visitor, the magnanimous faces of the Bodhisattva Avalokiteshvara staring out over the kingdom. Imagine being a peasant in the 13th century, approaching the forbidding capital for the first time. It would have been an awe-inspiring yet unsettling experience to enter such a gateway and come face to face with the divine power of the god-kings.

The last great capital of the Khmer empire, Angkor Thom took monumental to a whole new level. It was built in part as a reaction to the surprise sacking of Angkor by the Chams – Jayavarman VII decided that his empire would never again be vulnerable at home. Beyond the formidable walls is a massive moat that would have stopped all but the hardiest invaders.

Right at the heart of the ancient city is Bayon, the mesmerising if slightly mind-bending state temple of Jayavarman VII. He was a new king and wanted to promote a new religion, so what better way to do it than with the strangest structure at Angkor, complete with 216 enigmatic faces keeping watch over the population? Bayon is one of the most fascinating temples at Angkor, the faces best experienced

THE ENIGMA OF JAYAVARMAN VII

A devout follower of Mahayana Buddhism, Jayavarman VII is a figure of many contradictions. The bas-reliefs at Bayon depict him presiding over battles of terrible ferocity, while statues of the king show him in a meditative, otherworldly aspect. His ambitious programme of temple building can be explained partly by a desire to legitimise his rule, and partly by the need to introduce a new religion to a predominantly Hindu population. In many ways he was also Cambodia's first socialist leader, proclaiming the population equal, abolishing castes and embarking on a programme of school, hospital and road building.

in the soft light of early morning or late afternoon. Still, you can't help but wonder what on earth Jayavarman was on. Some pretty strong stuff, one imagines.

Beyond Bayon lies a collection of creations that are similarly impressive. Baphuon would undoubtedly have been one of the most inspired temples in its heyday, but is now better known as the world's largest jigsaw puzzle (see p74). Nearby are the remains of the royal palace compound, fronted by the Terrace of Elephants, the king's royal viewing gallery to take in the pomp and pageantry of his reign. Several of the smaller sites – including captivating Preah Palilay, a late-Buddhist temple sheltered by a cluster of kapok trees – see few visitors.

See p67 for more information.

>3 TONLÉ SAP LAKE

WALK ON WATER IN THE FLOATING VILLAGES

Tonlé Sap lake may be a miracle of nature (see p96), but the floating villages that dot the lake are also out of this world. Whole villages, sometimes small towns, bob on the surface of the lake, their livelihoods dependent on the freshwater fish catch. Everything floats in these communities: the school, the health centre, the petrol station, the general stores, the karaoke bars, even the livestock in the form of crocodiles and pigs (although hopefully not in the same cage). Some houses float on platforms with giant fish nets spread beneath, ensuring a meal is never far away. Others are precariously strung across three boat hulls and barely weather the storms that sometimes whip across the lake.

Chong Kneas (p93) is the most popular of the floating villages near Siem Reap. The village migrates with the movement of the water: in the wet season it lies just 11km from Siem Reap; in the dry

season it might be 15km or more away. Rent a boat and explore the 'side streets' of this major village, or take in a sunset from a rooftop restaurant on the lake.

Kompong Phhluk (p94) doesn't technically float, although it might appear that way if you are visiting in September. Visit in the dry season and the secret is revealed, as these houses are built on skinny stilts to keep them above the rising waters. Nearby is a flooded, almost amphibious forest, able to survive above and below the water and best explored by canoe.

Further afield are dozens more villages, and it's possible to visit some of the smaller ones on an ecotourism adventure to Prek Toal Bird Sanctuary (p92), about 40km southwest of Siem Reap. Home to some of the world's rarest large water birds, Prek Toal is an impressive experience for casual observers as well as serious bird-watchers. The floating villages here are engaged in handicraft production to help establish a sustainable income that doesn't disturb the delicate balance of nature.

>4 JUNGLE TEMPLES

FOLLOW IN THE FOOTSTEPS OF THE EXPLORERS OF OLD

While Angkor Wat flourished – converted to a Buddhist shrine and venerated by generations of pilgrims – the other temples around Angkor were abandoned to the elements. Vines and creepers embraced the *apsaras* (heavenly nymphs); tree roots throttled the temples in their thirst for water. So hidden was the ancient capital of Angkor Thom that King Ang Chan stumbled across it by accident when on a hunting trip near Angkor Wat in the 16th century. Portuguese explorers were the first Europeans to visit the temples, but it wasn't until the 19th century that Angkor exploded onto the world stage, when Henri Mouhot's account of his 'discovery' was published.

There may have been millions more visitors since then, but it is still possible to experience the awe of the first explorers. Iconic Ta Prohm (p79) is the original jungle temple of Angkor, left by conservationists as a testament to the force of nature. Ancient corridors groan under the weight of immense trees, the root systems slowly and stealthily strangling the life out of the stones. Further afield lies Beng Mealea (p99), a prototype for Angkor Wat that was swallowed by the voracious jungle. Here is the authentic atmosphere of the abandoned temple, and beyond lie hundreds of smaller structures awaiting discovery.

>5 CULINARY DELIGHTS
SAVOUR THE FLAVOURS, FROM STREET STALLS TO GOURMET RESTAURANTS

Siem Reap has emerged from the dark ages and transformed itself into a 21st-century dining destination. That said, this is Cambodia and the dark ages were more about turmoil than a lack of good food: even the simplest stalls in this town can turn out tasty creations. To sample the local flavours, do some street surfing along Sivatha St (p41), hunker down at Psar Chaa (p40) or eat on the run around the temples (p56).

Classier Khmer cuisine is also available in abundance, and many of the better places are set in atmospheric traditional wooden houses draped in silks and finery: try Sugar Palm (p41), Madame Butterfly (p55) or Café Indochine (p37). Or be brave and cook your own croc or snake steak at Cambodian BBQ (p37).

A new generation of culinary crusaders is travelling the world, breaking rules and conventions to create something new. Blending the best of Cambodia with the rest of the world, the results are refreshing. Try L'Escale des Arts & des Sens (p40) or Aha (p35).

There are also chic cafés like Blue Pumpkin (p36); top French restaurants like Le Malraux (p39) and Damnak Alliance Café (p38); and restaurants doing their bit to help Cambodia, like Butterflies Garden Restaurant (p37), Sala Bai (p40) and the Singing Tree Café (p40). Temples schmemples: food is yet one more reason to extend your stay.

>6 CLASSICAL DANCE

SEE THE APSARAS OF ANGKOR COME TO LIFE

Cambodia's classical dance is a living link to the glories of the Angkor period, when young maidens danced as messengers of the gods. Witness a dance spectacle today and there will be almost as many costumes and hair styles on show as there are on the beautiful *apsaras* at Angkor Wat. The origins of classical dance may be Indian, but over centuries it has been refined into a uniquely Cambodian art form.

The Hindu epic *Ramayana,* known as the *Reamker* in Cambodia, features prominently. Some of the more extravagant dances include re-enactments of the battles between Hanuman and the demon-king Ravana, as well as the Churning of the Ocean of Milk.

The Khmer Rouge's assault on the arts was a terrible blow to Khmer culture. Destroying anything that served as a reminder of a past it was trying to efface, the Khmer Rouge killed off many of the living bearers of culture, including classical dancers and musicians.

Tourism has played its part in the resurgence of classical dance, and there are now lots of restaurants around Siem Reap offering dinner and dance shows. Best value is the nightly show at Temple Club (p45), but for more salubrious surroundings try the Dining Room (p44) or Apsara Theatre (p44). There are also occasional spectacles around Angkor, complete with light-and-sound shows. Look out for the French-coordinated Les Nuits d'Angkor, usually some time around Christmas and New Year.

Statue of the Hindu deity, Vishnu

ITINERARIES

To get the most out of Angkor's magnificent monuments, plotting a course is essential. The A-list attractions include the one and only Angkor Wat, the slightly spooky faces of Bayon, and iconic Ta Prohm. The heat will take its toll, so don't be over-ambitious: Angkor is best savoured, not rushed.

ONE DAY

Are you mad? One day is not enough to do Angkor justice, but if that's all you have, make the most of it. See Angkor Wat (p60) at sunrise, then stick around to explore the mighty temple when the crowds are light. Continue to the tree roots of Ta Prohm (p79) before breaking for lunch. In the afternoon, explore the walled city of Angkor Thom (p67), admiring the bizarre beauty of Bayon.

TWO DAYS

Two days allows time to include some of the big hitters around Angkor. Spend the first morning visiting petite Banteay Srei (p98), with its fabulous carvings; visit the Cambodia Land Mine Museum (p50) to learn about these insidious inventions; and see Banteay Samré (p88). In the afternoon, visit immense Preah Khan (p83), delicate Preah Neak Poan (p85) and the strangler fig of Ta Som (p86), before taking in sunset at Pre Rup (p87). Spend the second day following the one-day itinerary above.

THREE TO FIVE DAYS

With three to five days to explore Angkor, it's possible to see most of the important sites. One school of thought is to see as much as possible on the first couple of days (as covered above) and then spend the final days visiting other sites such as Roluos (p96) and Banteay Kdei (p79), as well as revisiting the stunners that caught your eye. Better still is a gradual build-up to the most spectacular monuments, progressing through minor temples first. Another original option is a chronological approach, starting with the earliest temples and working forwards in time to Angkor Thom, taking stock of the evolution of Khmer architecture along the way.

Top left An ancient stupa at Preah Khan (p83) **Bottom left** Feasting on the bank of the river

It's worth making the trip to the River of a Thousand Lingas at Kbal Spean (p101), offering the chance to stretch your legs amid natural and man-made splendour, or visiting the vast and overgrown temple of Beng Mealea (p99). There's also the chance to veer away from the temples and experience life on the water at one of the floating villages of Tonlé Sap lake (p93 and p94), or to enjoy one of the many activities on offer, such as quad biking (p53), horse riding (p52) or cooking classes (p33).

ONE WEEK

Those with the time to spend a week at Angkor will be richly rewarded. Not only is it possible to see all the temples of the region, but a longer stay also allows for relaxing by a pool, indulging in a spa treatment or shopping around Siem Reap. Check out the aforementioned itineraries for some ideas, but relax in the knowledge that you'll see it all. It's also worth tackling an adventure to a more remote site, such as Koh Ker (p102) or Prek Toal Bird Sanctuary (p92).

Temple-trekking can be tiring work...recuperate with a foot massage (p116)

FORWARD PLANNING

Gone are the days when friends would look at you with a mix of concern and confusion, muttering 'oh, so you're going to Cambodia?' And gone too are the days when you had to plan things way in advance, as it's easy enough to turn up and tune in straight from the plane.

Four weeks before you go If you are visiting during the high season (November to March), plan ahead and book a room. Start swotting up on the temples and working out which places you want to visit at what time of day to dodge the crowds, and pick up some books on the messy modern history of Cambodia.

Two weeks before you go Anyone planning to travel overland from Thailand can arrange an e-Visa (see p132) to prevent overcharging at the border. If you want a more structured tour of the temples, think about booking a tour guide to lead the way. Take a look at the wining and dining scene and work out where you plan to party.

The day before you go Play hunt-the-passport. Bid farewell to friends over a favourite tipple. Double check which airport you're flying out of before you book a ride. Dream of the world's most magnificent temples.

THE TEMPLES ON TWO WHEELS

Angkor is a great area for exploring by bicycle, as this is the perfect way to slow things down and meet the locals. Cycling around the main temples is pretty straightforward and it's easy enough to follow the one- or two-day itinerary outlined above. To see a bit more of the countryside, take in some back roads. Consider cycling to Roluos (p96) along the country trails from Wat Dam Nak, or cycle through the village of Preah Dak to Banteay Samré (p88) before looping back via NH6. Another option is to cycle out to the Western Baray (p88) and enter Angkor Thom via the West Gate, like the locals from nearby villages.

Children performing traditional Khmer dance, Siem Reap

>SIEM REAP CENTRE

Gateway to the eighth wonder of the world, Siem Reap (*see*-em ree-*ep*) was always destined for greatness. Back in the day, a steady stream of literati and socialites sidled through, including Somerset Maugham and Charlie Chaplin, but as Cambodia imploded into war and genocide, Siem Reap went into a state of suspended animation for three decades. Well, it's woken up and is making up for lost time.

The French provided the blueprint for central Siem Reap, with its tree-lined boulevards and old shophouses. The social hub is Psar Chaa (Old Market), where there are dangerous diversions for shopaholics. Nearby Sivatha St is the closest thing to a High St. The riverside area is more sedate and includes a selection of hotels and eating options. It merges into the temple district of Wat Bo, with budget digs and eats to suit every wallet.

SIEM REAP CENTRE

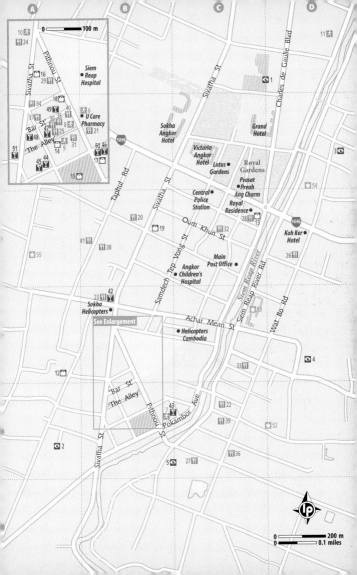

Enlargement

0   100 m

10 🔺
24 ▽

Pithnou St

16
29 ▽

Siem
Reap
Hospital

Sivatha St

34 ▽

18 ▽
49 ▽   40
30   35
8   25
47 ▽
48 ▽   27

6 ▽
U Care
Pharmacy

'Bar St'

21 ▽

44
45 ▽
Y

'The Alley'
31
14
4

51 ▽
Y

50   46
17 ▽

15 ▽

NH6

Main Map

11 🔺

Charles de Gaulle Blvd

Sivatha St

1 🔄

Sokha
Angkor
Hotel

Grand
Hotel

Victoria
Angkor
Hotel

Lotus •
Gardens

Royal
Gardens

3 🔄

Prasat •
Preah
Ang Charm

54 ⭐

Central •
Police
Station

Royal •
Residence

Oum Khun St

32 ▽

28 ▽ 13

Koh Ker •
Hotel

NH6

Taphul Rd

20 ▽

19 ▽

Siem Reap River

26 ▽

41 ▽   38 ▽

55 ⭐

Samdech Tep Vong St

Angkor •
Children's
Hospital

Main
Post Office

Siem Reap River Rd

Wat Bo Rd

23 ▽   42
Y

Sokha •
Helicopters

See Enlargement

Achar Mean St

Helicopters •
Cambodia

18

12 ▽

4 🔄

33 ▽

2 🔄

'Bar St'

'The Alley'

Pithnou St

Pokambor Ave

43
Y

22 ▽

39 ▽

52 ⭐

Sivatha St

5 🔄   27 ▽

36 ▽

0   200 m
0   0.1 miles

◉ SEE

◉ ANGKOR NATIONAL MUSEUM

☎ 063-966601; www.angkornational
museum.com; 968 Charles de Gaulle Blvd;
admission US$12, children under 1.2m
US$6; ⏱ 6am-6pm

A state-of-the-art showcase for the
Khmer civilisation and the majesty
of Angkor, with displays themed
by era, religion and royalty.
Presentations include touchscreen
video and epic commentary, but
for all the technology there seems
to be a scarcity of sculpture – a
triumph of style over substance.
It seems a touch overpriced, but
remains a useful initiation for first-
time visitors to put the story of the
Khmer empire in context.

◉ ARTISANS D'ANGKOR

☎ 063-380354; www.artisansdangkor
.com; west of Sivatha St; admission free;
⏱ 7.30am-5.30pm

Siem Reap is the epicentre of the
drive to revitalise Cambodian culture, which was dealt such a harsh
blow by the Khmer Rouge. Les
Chantiers Écoles runs this school
specialising in teaching wood- and
stone-carving techniques to im-
poverished youngsters. Tours are
available daily. The site includes
a shop, selling reproduction carvings, lacquerware and exquisite
silks, and profits from sales go
back into funding the school.

WHAT'S IN A NAME?

The name Siem Reap means 'Siamese
Defeated', hardly the most tactful name
for a major city near Thailand. Imagine
Birmingham with the name Germany
Defeated! The empire of Angkor once
included much of modern-day Thailand,
but there's a touch of irony about the
name, given that Thailand ultimately
defeated Cambodia, and controlled Siem
Reap and Angkor from 1794 to 1907.

◉ MINIATURE REPLICAS OF ANGKOR'S TEMPLES

east bank of river; admission US$1.50;
⏱ 6am-6pm

Can't afford the helicopter ride
over Angkor? Don't fancy the
balloon? For the bluffer's way
to get that aerial shot of Angkor
Wat, visit the garden of a local
master sculptor, which houses
miniature replicas of Angkor Wat,
the Bayon, Banteay Srei and
other temples. Astute observers
might question the presence
of oversized insects in the
shot, and it doesn't quite
deliver the authentic sunrise
over Angkor.

◉ WAT BO

Wat Bo Rd; admission free; ⏱ 6am-6pm

Wat Bo is one of the town's oldest
temples. It has a collection of
well-preserved wall paintings
from the late-19th century, depicting the *Reamker*, Cambodia's

Srei Omnoth
Tour guide

How long have you been a tour guide? I started back in 1995. **What is your favourite temple at Angkor?** That's a hard question. I love Ta Prohm (p79) for its undiscovered feel, as it shows visitors an abandoned temple claimed by the jungle. **What is your favourite Cambodian dish?** *Tuk kreung*, a country broth made from fermented fish and special herbs and spices. **What is your favourite tipple?** I am sure I am supposed to say Angkor Beer, but actually I prefer Tiger Beer. **Which tourists do you like to look after?** I like the Americans as they are generous tippers and I like the British thanks to their ancient history. Stonehenge particularly interests me thanks to its alignment with the constellations, like Angkor. **Where would you most like to visit?** The Himalayas as the birthplace of Buddhism, or the UK for its history, to see Westminster Abbey and other landmarks.

Quiet reflection at Wat Bo (p30)

interpretation of the *Ramayana*. Look out for the stunning roof of the main pagoda, a classical Khmer design.

◉ WAT DAM NAK
east bank of river; admission free; ☷ **6am-6pm**

This pretty compound was formerly a royal palace during the reign of King Sisowath, hence the name *dam nak* (palace). Today it is home to the **Centre for Khmer Studies** (www.khmerstudies.org), an independent institution promoting a greater understanding of Khmer culture with a drop-in library on site.

🏃 DO
🏃 BODIA SPA
☎ **063-761593; Pithnou St;** ☷ **10am-midnight**

A sophisticated spa near Psar Chaa offering a full range of scrubs, rubs and natural remedies, including its own line of herbal products made from Cambodian plant extracts.

🏃 BODYTUNE
☎ **063-764141; Pokambor Ave; massage US$12-37;** ☷ **10am-10pm**

Pamper that inner princess at this lavish outpost of a leading Thai spa. This is a fine place to relax and unwind on the riverfront,

FACE IT
Getting to grips with face is the key to success in Asia, and Cambodia is no exception. Having 'big face' is synonymous with prestige, and prestige is important in Cambodia. Getting angry, shouting or becoming abusive is impolite; it means loss of face and makes all Asians uncomfortable. Take a deep breath and keep your cool. If things aren't being done as they should, remember that there is a shortage of skilled people in the country because the majority of educated Cambodians either fled the country or were killed between 1975 and 1979.

set in a grand old French-era building.

🏃 COOKS IN TUK TUKS
☎ 063-963400; www.therivergarden
.info; east bank of river; courses US$18-25;
🕙 departs 10am
Hit the road by tuk tuk and visit Psar Leu market, before returning to the peaceful River Garden for a professional introduction to the secrets of Cambodian cooking.

🏃 DR FEET
☎ 063-965034; Pithnou St;
massage US$5-10; 🕙 10am-late
It would take a brave sole to argue with Dr Feet's credentials. Exploring the vast temple complexes takes its toll on the toes and this is the place to restore the balance before another day of adventures.

🏃 FRANGIPANI
☎ 063-964391; The Alley; 🕙 10am-10pm
Located down the narrow alley between Psar Chaa and Bar St, this delightful little retreat offers

massage and a whole range of spa treatments.

🏃 LE TIGRE DE PAPIER COOKING SCHOOL
☎ 063-760930; www.letigredepapier
.com; Bar St; courses US$11;
🕙 starts 10am
This half-day cooking course is for a great cause, as all proceeds go to support the Sala Bai Hotel and Restaurant School, which trains disadvantaged Cambodians. Learn to bargain for vegetables in the market before whipping them into something aromatic and delicious.

🏃 SEEING HANDS MASSAGE 4
☎ 012 836487; 324 Sivatha St;
massage from US$5 per hr;
🕙 8am-9pm
You may well need a massage if you have been exploring the rollercoaster roads of upcountry Cambodia. This place deserves support, as it trains blind people in the art of massage.

COOKING THE CAMBODIAN WAY

Done the cooking course? Remember the tricks of the trade by picking up a Cambodian cookbook to take home. For the scoop on countryside cooking, seek out *From Spiders to Waterlilies*, a cookbook produced by Romdeng restaurant in Phnom Penh. Also check out *The Best of Friends*, a visual feast showcasing the best recipes from the capital's phenomenally popular Friends restaurant. Longteine De Monteiro runs several Cambodian restaurants on the east coast of the US, and has put together her favourite traditional Khmer recipes at www.elephantwalk.com.

SHOP

ANGKOR NIGHT MARKET
Market

near Sivatha St; 4pm-midnight
Something different on the Siem Reap shopping scene, this lively night market includes handicrafts, souvenirs and silks. Shopping by night is a great way to avoid tropical torpor, plus there is the Island Bar at the back of the market for a spot of libation.

JASMINE *Fashion*
☎ 063-760610; Pokambor Ave;
9am-10pm
Located in FCC Angkor, this designer emporium specialises in elegant evening wear and sartorial silk. The accent is hip if a little haughty and the designs suit all ages.

MCDERMOTT GALLERY
Photography
☎ 092 668181; www.mcdermottgallery .com; The Alley; 10am-10pm
This photography gallery is home to John McDermott's striking sepia-style images of the temples. For a preview of the temples in a different light, check out his online collection.

PSAR CHAA *Market*
near Sivatha St; 6am-9pm
Located in the heart of old Siem Reap, Psar Chaa (Old Market) is well stocked with anything you might want to buy in Cambodia (and lots of things you don't want to buy!). Silverware, silk, wood carvings, stone carvings, Buddhas, paintings, rubbings, T-shirts, table mats…the list is endless. There are bargains to be had if you haggle patiently and humorously.

RAJANA *Handicrafts*
☎ 063-964744; Sivatha St;
9am-9pm, closed Sun
This quirky little boutique offers original wooden and metalware objects, some hewn from the shells of decommissioned weapons. It also has smart silver jewellery and a delightful selection of handmade cards. Rajana promotes fair trade.

REHAB CRAFT
Silk, Handicrafts
☎ 063-380355; Pithnou St;
🕙 10am-7pm
One of the longest-running shops for a cause, Rehab Craft has a striking selection of silk in every shape and size, including wallets, handbags, ties and more. Profits train and sustain the disabled community.

SAMATOA
Tailor-Made Clothing
☎ 012 285930; Sivatha St;
🕙 8am-11pm
If you suddenly find yourself in need of a party frock, this designer dress shop offers original threads in silk, with the option of a tailored fit in 48 hours. Samatoa promotes fair trade.

SENTEURS D'ANGKOR
Scents, Spices
☎ 063-964860; Pithnou St;
🕙 8.30am-9.30pm
Opposite Psar Chaa, this shop has an eclectic collection of silk and carvings, as well as a superb range of traditional beauty products and spices, all sourced locally. It's also possible to visit the production line just outside Siem Reap, a sort of Willy Wonka's for the senses.

TABITHA CAMBODIA
Silk, Handicrafts
Sivatha St; 🕙 7am-6pm
This cosy little shop stocks silk scarves, cushion covers and throws, as well as an original selection of soft toys. Proceeds go towards community-aid projects like house-building and well-drilling.

🍴 EAT
🍴 ABACUS
French, European $$
☎ 012 644286; off Sivatha St;
🕙 11am-late
The setting in a traditional wooden house belies a sophisti-cated menu of French-accented creations. The selection combines Gallic classics like entrecôte and duck breast with new-world additions like ostrich and smoked salmon. By night, barflys sip drinks around the counter.

🍴 AHA
International $-$$
☎ 063-965501; The Alley;
🕙 7am-11pm
Forget fusion food – that is so passé these days. This is a fusion restaurant, launched by several leading designer-hotels and the McDermott Gallery. It literally opened its doors as we were in town and offers top-notch tapas

SIEM REAP & AROUND

SIEM REAP CENTRE

Grab a bite to eat at funky fusion restaurant AHA (p35)

and lighter bites, a fine wine list and free wi-fi.

🍴 AMOK *Khmer* $$
☎ 012 800309; The Alley; ⏲ 5-11pm
Paying homage to the national dish of Cambodia, *amok* (a delectable baked fish curry in banana leaf), this smart pavement diner offers traditional Khmer fare. Try *amok* in four flavours or savour the scented salads and aromatic soups.

🍴 ANGKOR PALM
Khmer $$
☎ 063-761436; Pithnou St;
⏲ 10am-10pm
Combining the authentic taste of Cambodian country cooking with Western attention to detail, the combination platter here is the perfect crash course in Khmer cuisine, with seven dishes (including fresh spring rolls and stir-fried morning glory) beautifully presented in banana leaves.

🍴 BLUE PUMPKIN
International $
☎ 063-963574; Pithnou St;
⏲ 6am-10pm
Downstairs it could be just another café, albeit with a delightful selection of cakes, breads, pastries and homemade ice cream. But head upstairs to find an old-school Starck (Philippe that is) interior, another world of white minimalist expression, with day beds that drain you of all will to leave. Light bites, filling specials, ice-cream creations and divine shakes – what more can you ask for? OK, there's also free wi-fi.

🍴 BUTTERFLIES GARDEN RESTAURANT
International $-$$
☎ 063-761211; east bank of river;
🕐 9am-10pm

This lush garden is home to more than 1000 butterflies that float above the tables, making it a hit with families. Khmer flavours, comfort food from home and indulgent desserts – take a flutter on something. Butterflies Garden supports local causes.

🍴 CAFÉ DE LA PAIX
International $-$$
☎ 063-966000; Hotel de la Paix, Sivatha St; 🕐 6am-10pm

Air-conditioning and free wi-fi make this the perfect bolt hole on a hot, sticky day, and what could be better than passion-fruit or mango ice cream to help cool off? Caffeine fiends will love the Lavazza coffee.

🍴 CAFÉ INDOCHINE
Khmer, Asian $$
☎ 012 804952; Sivatha St; 🕐 10am-3pm & 5-11pm

Once upon a time, all the houses in Siem Reap looked like this, but only a few traditional wooden structures remain. Popular with tour groups, and for good reason, this atmospheric place offers fragrant Khmer and Asian food. There's air-con downstairs, and a healthy wine cellar.

🍴 CAMBODIAN BBQ
Khmer, International $$
☎ 063-965407; The Alley; 🕐 dinner

Long a Cambodian favourite, the traditional *phnom pleung* (hill of fire) is a DIY tabletop barbecue of meat or seafood. Here they take it to another level by introducing exotic meats, including crocodile, snake (if you dare), ostrich and kangaroo.

🍴 CHIVIT THAI *Thai* $-$$
☎ 012 830761; 130 Wat Bo Rd;
🕐 7am-10pm

Get down with Thai cuisine on the inviting floor cushions here, or choose table dining if the back is refusing to bend. The most alluring

---

FISHY BUSINESS FOR VEGETARIANS

Few Cambodians understand the concept of strict vegetarianism, and many will say something is vegetarian to please the customer when in fact things are a bit fishier than that. If you are not a strict vegetarian and can deal with fish sauces and the like, you should have few problems ordering meals. In Siem Reap, many of the international restaurants feature vegetarian dishes. Indian restaurants can cook up genuine vegetarian food, as they usually understand the principles better than the *prahoc* (fermented fish paste)-loving Khmers.

of the Thai restaurants in town, it is set in a beautiful wooden villa. All the classics are here, including a delicious *laab* (spicy Thai salad with fish or meat).

🍴 DAMNAK ALLIANCE CAFÉ
French, Asian $$-$$$
☎ 063-964242; Wat Dam Nak area;
🕑 10am-10pm
This classy French restaurant also pays homage to its Cambodian context, with starters that include a rare lotus-salad. Try scallops on a bed of spinach and graduate to duck breast in a passion-fruit sauce, but remember to save room for the desserts.

🍴 FCC ANGKOR
International, Asian $$-$$$
☎ 063-760280; Pokambor Ave;
🕑 7am-midnight
OK, so it's never been a foreign correspondents' club, but you'd never know when sipping a planter's punch in the lounge chairs of the colonial-chic bar. This bold building has a magnetic impact on riverside strollers thanks to a reflective pool, torchlit dining and a garden bar. The open kitchen turns out a range of Asian and international food.

🍴 GINGA *Japanese* $$-$$$
☎ 063-963366; off Charles de Gaulle Blvd; 🕑 lunch & dinner

The Siem Reap outpost of one of Phnom Penh's finest Japanese restaurants, Ginga does a roaring trade with Japanese visitors – always a good sign. The menu includes some sashimi and sushi sets, plus cheaper combo boxes.

🍴 HAPPY HERB'S PIZZA
Italian $-$$
☎ 092 838134; Pithnou St; 🕑 7am-11pm
No, happy doesn't mean free toppings; it means pizza à la ganja that leaves diners on a high. Choose from happy or extra happy, but proceed with caution if you don't want to write off the rest of your day. Nonhappy pizzas also available.

🍴 KAMA SUTRA *Indian* $$
☎ 017 824474; Bar St; 🕑 noon-late; Ⓥ
It's not just the name that's sexy here, as this stylish Indian restaurant serves sensual flavours that hit the spot every time. All the heavyweights are here, including tikka masala, daal and creamy curry, and there are regional specialities from north and south.

🍴 KHMER KITCHEN RESTAURANT *Khmer, Asian* $
☎ 063-964154; The Alley;
🕑 11am-10pm; Ⓥ
Can't get no culinary satisfaction? Just follow in the footsteps of Sir Mick to this back-alley stalwart

that kick-started life between the streets. Khmer and Thai favourites make up the menu, which includes a generous vegetarian selection based around pumpkin or sweet potato.

LE CAFÉ *International* $

☎ 092 271392; Wat Bo area;
🕑 7.30am-9pm

It couldn't be anything but cultured thanks to its location in the French Cultural Centre, but its partnership with the Paul Dubrule Hotel & Tourism School (see Les Jardins des Delices, right) means it's also for a good cause. Enjoy five-star sandwiches, salads and shakes from the Sofitel school of hospitality.

LE MALRAUX
French $$-$$$

☎ 063-966041; Sivatha St;
🕑 7am-midnight

The Art Deco atmosphere here could be a throwback to Cambodia's golden age before the civil war. Great for gastronomes, the fine French food includes a combination salmon *tartare* and *carpaccio* that melts in the mouth.

LE TIGRE DE PAPIER
International, Italian $-$$

☎ 063-760930; www.letigredepapier
.com; Bar St; 🕑 24hr

Le Tigre has a split personality, facing onto both busy Bar St and the

more sedate Alley. By day it's all about food, which includes professional pizzas, homemade pasta, a nod to mainland Europe and some local specialities. By night there's a big screen and the 24-hour kitchen quells the midnight munchies.

LES JARDINS DES DELICES
French, International $$

☎ 063-963673; Paul Dubrule Hotel & Tourism School, NH6 west; 🕑 noon-2pm Mon-Fri

A training restaurant established by Accor founder Paul Dubrule, this is the smart setting to experience Sofitel style at a snip. The set menu includes a selection of French or Asian dishes for just US$8.

🍽 LES ORIENTALISTES
Khmer, French $$
☎ 063-760278; 613 Wat Bo Rd;
🕐 lunch & dinner

Oozing the essence of the Orient, this exotic restaurant is decorated with Middle Eastern carpets, voluptuous archways and stylish hangings. It serves a balanced blend of Khmer, French and Moroccan cuisine, including tasty tapas.

🍽 L'ESCALE DES ARTS & DES SENS
Khmer, International $$-$$$
☎ 063-761442; www.escale-arts-sens .com; Oum Khun St; 🕐 6.30am-10pm

Created to celebrate the senses, this striking villa promotes renowned French chef Didier Corlou's new Asian cuisine. The sumptuous tapas platters are a must and include a selection of teasing tasters, all washed down with a dash of rice wine. Mains include beef cooked seven ways, inspired by a royal recipe for tiger meat (thankfully not on the menu).

🍽 PSAR CHAA STALLS
Khmer $
north side of Psar Chaa; 🕐 7am-9pm

Duck into the market and dip into the pots and pans bubbling and simmering with flavour. Cheap and cheerful, this is the real taste of Cambodia and locals flock here too. Try *kor chrrouk* (braised pork

in sugar palm) or *samlor m'chouu* (hot-and-sour soup).

🍽 RED PIANO
International $-$$
☎ 063-963240; Bar St; 🕐 7am-11.30pm

Packed to the rafters every night, the Red Piano has long been popular. Set in a grand colonial-era building in the heart of town, it has a broad balcony that's perfect for people-watching. The menu is East meets West, with some Khmer, Asian and Indian dishes squaring off against the European heavyweights. Former celebrity guest Angelina Jolie has a cocktail named in her honour.

🍽 SALA BAI
Khmer, International $
☎ 063-963329; www.salabai.com; Ta Phul Rd; 🕐 noon-2pm Mon-Fri

Sala Bai was doing the Jamie Oliver thing long before Jamie opened the doors to fashionable Fifteen. This training school introduces disadvantaged young Khmers to the art of hospitality and you're the guinea pig. The small menu includes Western and Khmer cuisine, plus a set lunch for US$5.

🍽 SINGING TREE CAFÉ
International $
☎ 063-965210; www.singingtreecafe .com; Wat Dam Nak area; 🕐 7.30am-9pm, closed Mon; Ⓥ

A delightful family-friendly café set in an expansive garden, this is the place for scrumptious muffins and health food, including a strong showing for vegetarians. It doubles as a community centre, yoga studio and gallery, committing a percentage of profits to good causes.

🍴 SIVATHA ST STALLS
Khmer $

Sivatha St; ⏱ **5pm-late**
Fast food, Khmer-style. These street stalls set up in the late afternoon and keep the fried rice and noodles coming until the early hours. Young Khmers come here to cast furtive, often flirtatious, glances at each other. The stalls can be a life-saver after a crawl along Bar St.

🍴 SOUP DRAGON
Khmer, International $-$$
☎ 063-964933; Bar St;
⏱ 6am-11pm; V

Start with classic Asian breakfasts on the ground floor, just the recipe before tackling the temples. Later in the day, venture upstairs to the smarter restaurant with a global menu. The rooftop bar donates a percentage of profits to the Angkor Children's Hospital, so drinking here is helping someone's liver, if not your own.

🍴 SUGAR PALM *Khmer* $$
☎ 063-964838; Ta Phul Rd;
⏱ 11am-late
This beautiful wooden house captures the spirit of Cambodia to perfection. With high ceilings, gentle breezes, polished *beng* (wood) floors and traditional decoration, the Sugar Palm is a place to sample traditional tastes infused with herbs and spices, including *char kreung* (spice paste) dishes with lemongrass and chilli.

EXPERIMENTAL (OR PLAIN MENTAL?) FOOD
Cambodia throws up food that is unusual, strange, maybe immoral or just plain weird. The fiercely omnivorous Cambodians find nothing strange in eating insects, algae, offal or fish bladders. They will dine on a duck foetus, brew up some brains or snack on some spiders. To the Khmers there is nothing 'strange' about anything that will sustain the body. To them food is either wholesome or it isn't; it tastes good or it doesn't. They'll try anything once, even a burger. We dare you to try one of the following:
> crickets – anyone for cricket?
> duck foetus – unborn duck, feathers and all
> durian – nasally obnoxious spiky fruit, banned on flights
> *prahoc* – fermented fish paste, almost a biological weapon
> spider – just like it sounds, a deep-fried tarantula

▽ DRINK

▽ ANGKOR WHAT? *Bar*

☎ 012 490755; Bar St; ⏰ 6pm-late

This is Siem Reap's original drinking dive, and the booze-addled graffiti that covers the walls is testament to its enduring popularity. The happy hour (to 8pm, with bargain buckets of Mekong whiskey and cheap Anchor pitchers) loosens up the limbs for later, when the crowd bounces along to indie anthems – some are on the tables, others under them.

▽ ARTS LOUNGE *Bar*

☎ 063-966000; Hotel de la Paix, Sivatha St; ⏰ 9am-11pm

A stylin' bar at the Hotel de la Paix, this contemporary art space plays host to challenging exhibitions. Cocktails are shaken to create a stir, and there are occasional celebrity bartenders and guest DJs from Bangkok.

▽ FUNKY MUNKY *Bar*

☎ 017 824553; www.funkymunky cambodia.com; Pokambor Ave; ⏰ noon-late, closed Mon

A Brit pub with a flair for food. Sample the brilliant build-your-own burgers, or try the slightly scary 'Cardiac Arrest'. There's truly funky décor, with artsy film posters, and a cocktail menu created for cheeky monkeys. Drop by on

---

BOTTOMS UP

When Cambodian men propose a toast, they usually stipulate what percentage must be downed. If they are feeling generous, it might be just *ha-sip pea-roi* (50%), but more often than not it's *moi roi pea-roi* (100%). This is why they love ice in their beer, as they can pace themselves over the course of the night. Many a *barang* (foreigner) has ended up face down on the table at a Cambodian wedding when trying to outdrink the Khmer boys without the aid of ice.

Thursday for the quiz; all proceeds are donated to local causes.

▽ IVY BAR *Bar*

☎ 012 800860; Psar Chaa area; ⏰ 6am-late

Commonly referred to as 'The Ivy', but no, it's not affiliated with its London namesake. One of the oldest bars in town, it does top pub grub and chilled draft beer. Look out for Pol Pot's toilet seat, pillaged from the ashes of Anlong Veng.

▽ JOE-TO-GO *Coffee Bar*

☎ 092 532640; www.theglobalchild.org; Psar Chaa area; ⏰ 5am-3pm

If you need coffee to course through your veins before you can muster the lustre for a sunrise at the temples, then sleepwalk your way here. Gourmet coffee, shakes and pastries, with proceeds supporting education and housing for street children.

▼ LAUNDRY BAR Bar
☎ 016 962026; Psar Chaa; ⏲ 6pm-late
Put on your cleanest undies and venture into one of the hippest bars in town. Low lighting, discerning décor and regular DJs are all crowd pleasers, and the pool table has them queuing up in the early hours. Happy hour lasts until 9pm.

▼ LINGA BAR Bar
☎ 012 246912; The Alley; ⏲ 5pm-late
A chic gay bar that pulls a straight crowd too, it wouldn't look out of place in London or New York. Now you know why you packed those

glam threads after all. Don them, order a cocktail and release that dancing diva within.

▼ MOLLY MALONE'S Bar
☎ 063-963533; Bar St;
⏲ 7.30am-midnight
If you're craving a Guinness, a Powers Whisky or a splash of stew, then this homely Irish pub is the place to come. Bringing the sparkle of the Emerald Isle to homesick Irish and a whole host of honorary Dubliners, it also hosts occasional live bands.

▼ TEMPLE CLUB Bar
☎ 015 999909; Bar St; ⏲ 10am-late
As the night wears on, the only worshipping going on at this

Hail the fine ale at the Temple Club (above)

temple is 'all hail the ale'. Loud tunes (often too loud) and some liberally minded local girls (some are actually boys) draw a dance crowd. Mad happy-hours from 10am to 10pm.

▼ WAREHOUSE Bar
☎ 063-965204; Pithnou St;
🕑 10.30am-3am

A popular bolt hole for expats escaping the madness of Bar St, this 'local' has lured many a traveller in for table football and indie anthems. The bar food is more cosmopolitan than most and best enjoyed from the 45-degree angle of a satellite chair. Free wi-fi.

▼ X BAR Bar
☎ 012 609680; Sivatha St;
🕑 4am-sunrise

X marks the spot for drunkards, dancers and those with a devilish twinkle in the eye. Just as everywhere else is winding down, the amps here are cranking up. There are early-evening movies on the

big screen, pool tables and a skateboard pipe – careful with the cocktails.

⭐ PLAY

⬛ APSARA THEATRE
Classical Dance
☎ 063-963561; Angkor Village, Wat Dam Nak area; admission US$25;
🕑 shows 6pm & 8pm

There are classical dance shows all over town, but the Apsara Theatre is a class apart, set in a striking wooden pavilion finished in the style of a wat, which plays host to one of the more renowned troupes around town. Sadly the set menu doesn't live up to the spectacle.

⬛ DINING ROOM
Classical Dance
☎ 063-963390; La Résidence d'Angkor, Siem Reap River Rd; free with dinner;
🕑 show 7.30pm Tue, Thu & Sat

A sophisticated restaurant at La Résidence, the Dining Room plays

---

SOMETHING FOR THE KIDDIES

Siem Reap is a great city for children these days, thanks to a range of activities beyond the temples. Many of the temples themselves will appeal to older children, particularly the Indiana Jones atmosphere of Ta Prohm and Beng Mealea, the sheer size and scale of Angkor Wat or the weird faces at the Bayon. However, try to limit the number of temples to the biggest and the best to ensure you don't experience a mutiny halfway through the tour.

Other popular activities include boat trips on Tonlé Sap lake (see Organised Tours, p139), exploring the countryside on horseback (see Happy Ranch, p52) or quad bike (see Quad Adventure Cambodia, p53), or goofing around at the Cambodian Cultural Village (p50).

For a taste of traditional culture, see a shadow puppet show

host to classical dance performances. Unlike at other high-flying hotels, you're not forced to buy an all-inclusive buffet. Offering fusion without confusion, the menu is creative yet classic.

⭐ LA NORIA *Shadow Puppets*
☎ 063-964242; La Noria Guesthouse, Siem Reap River Rd; admission US$12; ⏱ show 7pm Wed

The art of shadow puppetry has a history as old as the temples. La Noria hosts a traditional performance, plus classical dance, including a set meal. Part of the admission fee is donated to Krousar Thmey (p53), a charity supporting local children. Someone once called it Punch and Judy in leather, but that sounds like an S&M fetish.

⭐ TEMPLE CLUB
Classical Dance
☎ 015 999909; Bar St; free with dinner; ⏱ show 7.30pm

Keen to catch some classical dance but don't fancy grazing in the buffet troughs around town?

YABA DABA DO? YABA DABA DON'T!

Watch out for *yaba*, the 'crazy' drug from Thailand, known rather ominously in Cambodia as *yama* (the Hindu god of death). Called ice or crystal meth back home, this is homemade methamphetamines. *Yama* is more addictive than users would like to admit, provoking powerful hallucinations, sleep deprivation and psychosis. Also be very careful about buying 'cocaine'. One look at the map and the distance between Colombia and Cambodia should be enough to make you dubious, but it's worse than that. Most of what is sold as coke is actually pure heroin and far stronger than smack back home. Bang this up your hooter and you are in serious trouble.

Then worship at the Temple, where there's a nightly show upstairs.

⭐ ZONE ONE *Nightclub*
☎ 012 912347; west of Ta Phul Rd;
🕐 6pm-late

Count the number of hotels and restaurants in town and it soon adds up to a whole lot of young people with increasing cash to splash. Zone One is the club where most of them head for a night on the town. A few Westerners drift in, but this is essentially about young Khmers letting their hair down.

WALKING TOUR

SIEM REAP STROLL

In its soul, Siem Reap remains a small town, and strolling through the backstreets reveals life at a slower pace. Start with a ride to the old brick temple of **Wat Preah Inkosei** (**1**; p52) for a look at the architecture before Angkor. Follow the sleepy riverside road south before crossing the second narrow bridge on the right, which leads to a local street market bursting with activity. Continue down the west bank of

Service with a smile at Psar Chaa market (p34)

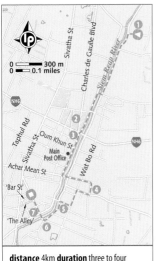

distance 4km **duration** three to four hours, with stops ▶ **start** Wat Preah Inkosei ● **end** Psar Chaa

the river until you reach the park, then cross the road to explore the beautiful **Royal Gardens (2)**, complete with fruit bats squawking in the trees. Follow the river road south, passing **FCC Angkor (3**; p38) and the post office. Cross the first bridge on the left, which leads to historic **Wat Bo (4**; p30) with its traditional frescoes. Continuing south on Wat Bo Rd, pop into **Butterflies Garden Restaurant (5**; p37) for a cold drink if it's a hot day. Follow the east bank of the river south until you reach **Wat Dam Nak (6**; p32), a former royal palace. Cross over the nearby bridge and explore the souvenir stalls of **Psar Chaa (7**; p34). If it's a morning stroll, enjoy lunch in one of the many cafés or restaurants around here; if it's late afternoon, try a tipple at one of the bars along the Alley or the aptly named Bar St.

>AROUND SIEM REAP

Siem Reap's suburbs are sprawling, as the town awakens and stretches from its slumber. When new hotels, restaurants, shops and spas open, so too do new satellite communities to absorb the human tide that is settling on the shores of Cambodia's boom town.

At first glance, NH6 west (aka Airport Rd) seems a jungle of giant hotels with little personality, but tucked away here are some romantic restaurants and sidetrack sights. Heading east on NH6 you'll find the Cambodian version of a strip mall, but Psar Leu is the real deal – a Cambodian market, warts and all.

More atmospheric are the quieter country suburbs. The road to the Tonlé Sap lake is lush and green, offering an accessible slice of village life. The road to Angkor is predictably overcrowded as everyone jockeys for a piece of the action, but down the side streets are rewarding restaurants and real life.

The area around Siem Reap is a world away from countryside Cambodia, but delivers the perfect blend of both worlds: comfort and sophistication on tap in town, with the chance to enjoy rural life.

AROUND SIEM REAP

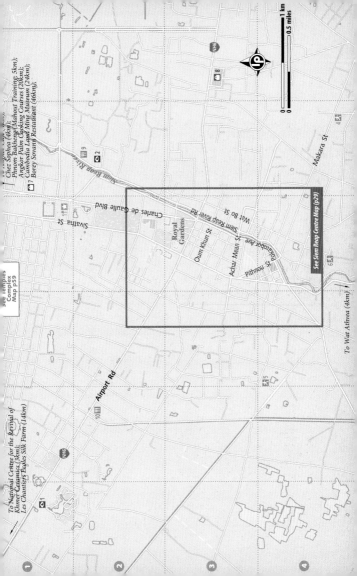

To National Centre for the Revival of
Khmer Ceramics (3km);
Les Chantiers Écoles Silk Farm (14km)

To Angkor Café (4km);
Chez Sophea (4km);
Phnom Bakheng (Mahout Training: 5km);
Cooking at the Sugar Palm (11km);
Cambodia Land Mine Museum (24km);
Borey Sovann Restaurant (46km)

See Temples
Complex
Map p59

Sivatha St

Charles de Gaulle Blvd

Royal
Gardens

Oum Khun St

Achar Mean St

Siem Reap River Rd

Wat Bo St

Pithnou St

Pokambor Ave

See Siem Reap Centre Map (p29)

Siem Reap River

Makara St

Airport Rd

To Wat Athvea (4km)

See Siem Reap Centre Map (p29)

See Temples Complex Map p59

1 km
0.5 miles

SEE

CAMBODIA LAND MINE MUSEUM

☎ 012 598951; www.cambodialand minemuseum.org; Banteay Srei district; admission US$1 donation; ⏱ 7am-6pm

Established by DIY de-miner Aki Ra, this museum has eye-opening displays on the curse of land mines in Cambodia. The collection includes mines, mortars, guns and weaponry, and there is a mock minefield where visitors can attempt to locate the deactivated mines. Proceeds from the museum are ploughed into mine-awareness campaigns. The museum is about 25km from Siem Reap, near Banteay Srei.

CAMBODIAN CULTURAL VILLAGE

☎ 063-963836; www.cambodiancultural village.com; Airport Rd; admission US$9, children under 1.1m free; ⏱ 8am-7pm

It may be kitsch, it may be kooky, but it is very popular with Cambodians and provides a diversion for families travelling with children. The visit begins with a wax museum and includes traditional homes of ethnic groups and miniature replicas of landmark Cambodian buildings. There are also dance shows and performances throughout the day.

LES CHANTIERS ÉCOLES SILK FARM

☎ 063-380354; www.artisansd angkor.com; admission free; ⏱ 7am-5pm

Les Chantiers Écoles maintains a silk farm where all stages of the production process, from the cultivation of mulberry trees to the dyeing and weaving of silk, can be seen. There is also a beautiful onsite boutique where silk creations are available. Free tours run daily and there's a free shuttle bus departing Artisans d'Angkor (p30) at 9.30am and 1.30pm. The farm is about 16km west of Siem Reap, near Puok.

NATIONAL CENTRE OF THE KHMER CERAMICS REVIVAL

☎ 063-761519; www.khmerceramics .com; near Airport Rd; admission free; ⏱ 8am-6pm

Dedicated to reviving the Khmer tradition of pottery, the centre has re-created an ancient Khmer kiln, which is helping to breathe new life into this old art. It's possible to try your hand at the potters wheel, and there are plenty of elegant items on sale. It's located near the airport.

WAT ATHVEA

admission free; ⏱ 6am-6pm

Wat Athvea is a pretty pagoda set on th'e site of an ancient

Khoem Bunloeurm
Buddhist monk, based at Wat Preah Inkosei (p52)

How long have you been a monk? It must be about eight years, as I was ordained when I was 20 and now I'm 28. **What led you to take up the robes?** First and foremost to become calm, but also to improve my studies, as monks get a discount at colleges. It is also a good way to research Cambodian literature, as I have learnt Pali and Sanskrit. **What is your favourite pagoda in Siem Reap?** If we talk about study and scholarship, then my favourite is Wat Dam Nak (p32). But the most important pagoda for the history of Buddhism is Wat Bo (p30) and it still supports living culture. **Where would you most like to go on a Buddhist pilgrimage?** It would have to be India, to see the birthplace of the Buddha and meditate in the places where he meditated. I would also love to meet the Dalai Lama.

sandstone temple that sees far fewer visitors than Angkor. It's south of the city centre, on the road to Tonlé Sap lake.

⊙ WAT PREAH INKOSEI
east bank of river; admission free;
☽ **6am-6pm**
Many modern pagodas were consecrated on the sacred ground of ancient temples. Wat Preah Inkosei is built on the site of an early Angkorian brick temple north of town; the older structure still stands at the rear of the compound.

⊙ WAT THMEI
Sivatha St; admission free; ☽ **6am-6pm**
Wat Thmei is a modern pagoda concealing a dark past, with a memorial stupa containing the bones of victims of the Khmer Rouge. There are plenty of young monks keen to practise their English here. It's located on the left fork of the road to Angkor Wat.

🏃 DO

🏃 ANGKOR GOLF RESORT
☎ **063-761139; www.angkor-golf.com; off Airport Rd;** ☽ **1st tee 7am, last tee 2.10pm**
This world-class course was designed by legendary British golfer Nick Faldo. Prices are also world-class, with green fees around US$100, plus more for a caddy, clubs and a cart.

🏃 ANGKOR PALM COOKING CLASSES
☎ **063-761436; www.angkorpalm.com; Banteay Srei district; classes from US$5**
A popular restaurant in Siem Reap, the Angkor Palm (p36) has opened a new wooden house near Banteay Srei temple, offering informal cooking classes at US$5 per dish.

🏃 AQUA
☎ **017 814010; www.aquacambodia.com; 7 Makara St; swimming US$2;** ☽ **9am-late**
If you are melting in the heat and don't have the benefit of a swimming pool at your hotel, head to Aqua, where there's a large pool and a lively little bar-restaurant.

🏃 HAPPY RANCH
☎ **012 920002; www.thehappyranch .com; south of Airport Rd; horse rides US$15-80**
Yee-haa, ride 'em cowboy! Explore Siem Reap on horseback, taking in surrounding villages and secluded temple spots. Riding lessons are also available for children and beginners.

🏃 MAHOUT TRAINING
☎ **063-963561; www.angkorvillage .com/elephants.php; Phnom Bakheng area; courses US$50**
A half-day mahout course (from 8am to midday) includes learning

some elephant commands, a ride around Angkor Thom and a chance to help bathe the elephant.

🚩 QUAD ADVENTURE CAMBODIA

☎ 092 787216; www.quad-adventure -cambodia.com; Wat Dam Nak area; rides US$19-76

Quad biking has come to Siem Reap and it's serious fun. Rides around Siem Reap include sunset over the ricefields, pretty temples or back roads through traditional villages where children wave manically. Quad Adventure Cambodia is well signposted in the Wat Dam Nak area.

🛍 SHOP

🛍 ERIC RAISINA WORKSHOP
Tailor-Made Clothing

☎ 063-965207; Wat Thmei area;
🕑 by appointment

Renowned designer Eric Raisina brings a unique cocktail of influences to his couture. Born in Madagascar, raised in France and resident in Cambodia, he offers a striking collection of clothing and accessories. Call ahead to arrange an appointment.

🛍 KROUSAR THMEY
Handicrafts, Puppets

☎ 063-964694; Charles de Gaulle Blvd;
🕑 8am-5.30pm

Part of an exhibition featuring life on Tonlé Sap lake, this small shop sells shadow puppets, traditional *krama* scarves, paintings and postcards. All proceeds go towards assisting blind or disadvantaged children in Cambodia.

🛍 PSAR LEU *Market*

NH6 east; 🕑 6am-6pm

If Psar Chaa draws the travel crowd on the hunt for trinkets,

KRAMA CHAMELEON

The colourful checked scarf known as the *krama* is almost universally worn by rural Khmers. The scarves are made from cotton or silk and there are some beautiful examples from the Phnom Srok area, about 90km northwest of Siem Reap. *Krama* have become very much a symbol of Cambodia and for many Khmers wearing one is an affirmation of their identity.

The *krama* is primarily used for protection from the elements, and this makes one a good investment. They are also slung around the waist as a mini-sarong, used as towels for drying the body, knotted at the neck as decorations, tied across the shoulders as baby carriers, used to tow broken-down motorbikes...the list goes on. *Krama* are sold in markets throughout Cambodia.

then Psar Leu (Upper Market) is where the locals come to shop. This vast complex offers pungent *prahoc* (fermented fish paste), fragrant fruits, household goods and anything else a Cambodian family might desire.

🍴 EAT

🍴 ANGKOR CAFÉ
International $

☎ 063-380300; opposite Angkor Wat;
🕑 10am-5.30pm

After slogging around the world's largest religious building, there's no better place to retreat than this café and gallery. The Blue Pumpkin (p36) looks after the menu, which includes homemade ice cream, fruit shakes, iced coffees and pastries, while Artisans d'Angkor (p30) take care of the handicrafts.

🍴 BOREY SOVANN *Khmer* $

☎ 063-760617; near Kbal Spean;
🕑 11am-2pm

Surely the farthest flung of the restaurants around Angkor, the peaceful garden retreat at Borey Sovann is a fine place to dine before or after a pilgrimage to the River of a Thousand Lingas at Kbal Spean.

🍴 CHEZ SOPHEA
French $$-$$$

☎ 012 858003; opposite Angkor Wat;
🕑 7am-9pm

In a superb spot opposite Angkor Wat, the unpretentious thatched roof belies a creative selection of barbecued meats and fish, accompanied by an original salad. Other options include homemade terrines and fiery apéritifs, making it popular with those in the know.

INCY WINCY SPIDER

One of Cambodia's more exotic culinary delights is the deep-fried spider: a big black tarantula smothered in oil and garlic. The creatures, decidedly dead, are piled high on platters, but don't get too complacent: there are usually live samples hidden in buckets nearby.

Spider is best treated like crab and eaten by cracking the body open and pulling the legs off one by one, bringing the juiciest flesh out with them. Alternatively, for a memorable photo, just bite the thing in half and hope for the best. Watch out for the abdomen, which can be filled with some pretty nasty-tasting brown sludge. It could be anything from eggs to excrement – spider truffles, perhaps?

Deep-fried spider snack – a culinary delight

L'OASI ITALIANA *Italian* $$
☎ 092 418917; Wat Preah Inkosei area;
⏰ 11am-2pm & 6-10pm,
closed Mon lunch

This really is an oasis, hidden away in a forest of trees near Wat Preah Inkosei. Local expats swear by the gnocchi and homemade pasta, rustled up by resident Italians.

MADAME BUTTERFLY
Khmer, Asian $$
☎ 016 909607; Airport Rd;
⏰ 6-11pm

In a traditional wooden house with sumptuous silks and billowing drapes, this restaurant offers Khmer dishes and a medley of Asian flavours. There are lots of quiet alcoves and hidden

corners for a romantic
night out.

🍜 TEMPLE STALLS *Khmer* $
🕐 6am-6pm

No-one goes hungry around
Angkor, as there are food stalls
at most major temples, serving
Khmer favourites and quick bites.
There are dozens of noodle stalls
just north of the Bayon; other
central temples where food is
available include Ta Prohm, Preah
Khan and Ta Keo. Further afield,
Banteay Srei, Kbal Spean and Beng
Mealea all have small restaurants
or food stalls.

⭐ PLAY

✪ BEATOCELLO *Classical music*
www.beatocello.com; Jayavarman VII
Children's Hospital, Charles de
Gaulle Blvd; 🕐 concerts 7.15pm
Thu & Sat

Dr Beat Richner's dynamic
musical alter-ego, Beatocello,
performs original and Bach cello
compositions in the conference
hall at Jayavarman VII Children's
Hospital. Entry is free, but dona-
tions are welcome, to assist the
hospital in offering free medical
treatment to the children
of Cambodia.

>THE TEMPLES OF ANGKOR

Young monk, Siem Reap

THE TEMPLES OF ANGKOR

Welcome to heaven on earth. Angkor is the earthly representation of Mt Meru, the Mt Olympus of the Hindu faith and the abode of ancient gods. The temples of Angkor, capital of Cambodia's ancient Khmer empire, are the perfect fusion of creative ambition and spiritual devotion.

Many visitors are surprised to find that Angkor is more than just its wat. Angkor Wat is so stupendous in stature that it eclipses everything else, but there's much more to see here. Visitors are staggered by the sheer scale of Angkor, the incredible volume of temples and the diversity in design from one era to another. Angkor has the epic proportions of the Great Wall of China, the detail and intricacy of the Taj Mahal and the symbolism and symmetry of the pyramids, all rolled into one.

The Cambodian god-kings of old each strove to better their ancestors in architectural expression, culminating in the last capital of Angkor Thom, a walled city that has to be seen to be believed. The hundreds of temples surviving today are but the sacred skeleton of the vast political, religious and social centre of an empire that stretched from Burma to Vietnam; a city that, at its zenith, boasted a population of one million when London was a small town of 50,000.

The temples of Angkor are the heart and soul of Cambodia, a source of inspiration and national pride to all Khmers as they struggle to rebuild their lives after years of terror and trauma.

ADMISSION FEES

Visitors have a choice of a one-day pass (US$20), a three-day pass (US$40) or a one-week pass (US$60). Passes cannot be extended and days run consecutively, so plan ahead. Passes include a digital photo snapped at the entrance booth, so the queues can be quite long. Visitors entering the monuments after 5pm get a free sunset, as the ticket starts from the following day. The fee includes access to all the monuments of Angkor in the Siem Reap area, but does not currently include Phnom Kulen, Beng Mealea or Koh Ker. Visitors found inside the central temples without a ticket will be fined US$100.

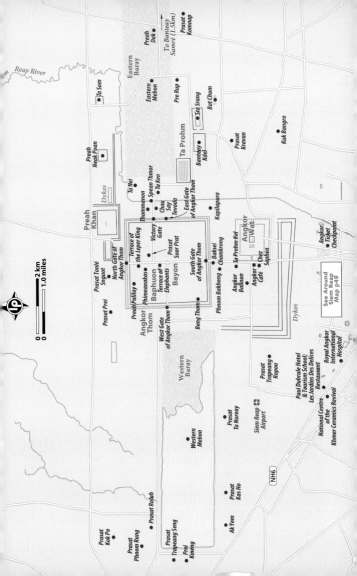

ANGKOR WAT

Simply put, there is nowhere else on earth quite like Angkor Wat. The largest and undoubtedly the most breathtaking of the monuments at Angkor, it is widely believed to be the largest religious structure in the world. This is hardly surprising given that its name means 'temple that is a city'. It is a stunning blend of spirituality and symmetry, an enduring example of man's devotion to his gods. Relish the very first approach, as that spine-tickling moment when you emerge on the inner causeway will rarely be felt again.

Angkor Wat is the best-preserved temple at Angkor, as it was never abandoned to the elements. It was probably built as a funerary temple for Suryavarman II (r 1112–1152) to honour Vishnu, the Hindu deity with whom the king identified.

There is much about Angkor Wat that is unique among the temples here. The most significant fact is that it is oriented towards the west, symbolically the direction of death, which led scholars to conclude that Angkor Wat must have existed as a tomb. Vishnu, however, is also frequently associated with the west, and it is most likely that Angkor Wat served both as a temple and a mausoleum for Suryavarman II.

A new day dawns at Angkor Wat

LAYOUT

Everything at Angkor Wat is epic in scale. The temple is surrounded by a 190m-wide moat, which forms a giant rectangle measuring 1.5km by 1.3km. From the west, a sandstone causeway crosses the moat. The sandstone blocks from which Angkor Wat was built were quarried more than 40km away near Phnom Kulen and floated down the Siem Reap River on rafts. According to inscriptions, the construction of Angkor Wat involved 300,000 workers and 6000 elephants, yet was still never completed.

The rectangular outer wall, measuring 1025m by 800m, has a gate on each side, but the main entrance, a 235m-wide porch richly decorated with carvings and sculptures, is on the western side. Look out for the statue of Vishnu, 3.25m in height and hewn from a single block of sandstone, located in the right-hand tower. You may see locks of hair lying about – these are offerings from young people preparing to get married, or pilgrims giving thanks for their good fortune.

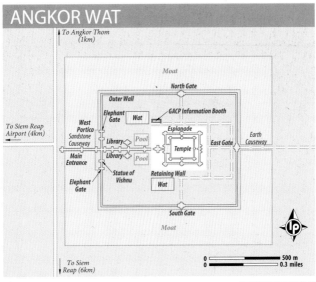

ANGKOR WAT

To Angkor Thom (1km)

Moat

North Gate

Outer Wall

Elephant Gate

Wat

GACP Information Booth

West Portico Sandstone Causeway

To Siem Reap Airport (4km)

Library

Pool

Esplanade

Temple

East Gate

Earth Causeway

Main Entrance

Library

Pool

Retaining Wall

Elephant Gate

Statue of Vishnu

Wat

South Gate

Moat

To Siem Reap (6km)

0   500 m
0   0.3 miles

An avenue, 475m long, 9.5m wide and lined with *naga* (serpent) balustrades, leads from the main entrance to the central temple, passing between two graceful libraries and then two pools, the northern one a popular spot from which to watch the sunrise.

The central temple complex consists of three storeys, which enclose a square surrounded by interlinked galleries. The Gallery of a Thousand Buddhas used to house hundreds of Buddha images before the war, but many of these were removed or stolen, leaving just a handful today.

The corners of the second and third storeys are marked by towers, each topped with symbolic lotus buds. Rising 31m above the third level and 55m above the ground is the central tower, which gives the whole ensemble its sublime unity. The stairs to the upper level are immensely steep, because pilgrims had to prostrate themselves in the presence of their gods.

Once at the central tower, the pilgrimage is complete: soak up the breeze, take in the views and then find a quiet corner in which to contemplate the symmetry and symbolism of this Everest of temples.

BAS-RELIEFS

Surely a candidate for the world's longest piece of art, the intricate and exquisite bas-reliefs of Angkor Wat wrap around the outer wall for almost 1km. It is impossible to imagine the work involved in creating such detail on this scale.

UNRAVELLING THE SYMBOLISM OF ANGKOR WAT

Visitors to Angkor Wat are struck by its imposing grandeur and its fascinating decorative flourishes. However, scholars and priests in the 12th century would have revelled in its multilayered levels of meaning in much the same way as a literary professor today might delight in James Joyce's *Ulysses*.

The spatial dimensions of Angkor Wat parallel the lengths of the four ages (Yuga) of classical Hindu thought. Thus the visitor to Angkor Wat who walks the causeway to the main entrance and through the courtyards to the final central tower is metaphorically travelling back to the first age of the creation of the universe.

Like the other temple-mountains of Angkor, Angkor Wat also replicates the spatial universe in miniature. The central tower is Mt Meru, with its surrounding smaller peaks, bounded in turn by continents (the lower courtyards) and oceans (the moat). The seven-headed *naga* becomes a symbolic rainbow bridge for man to reach the abode of the gods. Angkor Wat is quite literally heaven on earth.

Dr Ang Choulean
Leading archaeologist and scholar on Cambodian history

What is the most important Khmer temple? Angkor Thom is the most striking and challenging for archaeologists as it was a living city, with humans and gods co-habiting there. **What is the most important archaeological site in Cambodia?** Sambor Prei Kuk is among the most important for its homogeneity, given the period, and its artistic style. **Who is the most important king in Cambodian history?** Suryavarman I, who had a real political vision which can be measured by the monuments he built, such as Preah Vihear and Wat Phu. **What is your position on the debate between romance and restoration at Ta Prohm?** It is a matter of balance. The trees are most impressive, but maintaining the monument is our duty. **Which other civilisation interests you greatly?** Japanese civilisation, as it is so different from Khmer civilisation, allowing me to better understand mine.

What follows is a brief description of the epic events that unfold on the main bas-reliefs. They are described in the order in which you'll come to them if you begin on the western side and keep the bas-reliefs to your left. The majority of the bas-reliefs were completed at the time of construction in the 12th century, but several inferior reliefs were added in the 16th century.

(A) BATTLE OF KURUKSHETRA

The southern portion of the west gallery depicts a bloody battle scene from the Hindu *Mahabharata* epic, in which the Kauravas (from the north) and the Pandavas (from the south) fight to the death. Infantry scrap it out on the lowest tier, with officers on elephant-back and chiefs depicted on the second and third tiers. Over the centuries, successive pilgrims have touched the carvings, giving them the polished look of black marble. The portico at the southwestern corner is decorated with beautiful sculptures representing characters from the *Ramayana*.

(B) ARMY OF SURYAVARMAN II

The remarkable western section of the south gallery is a glimpse into life under the god-kings of Angkor. It depicts a triumphal battle-march of Suryavarman II's army. In the southwestern corner, look out for Suryavarman II on an elephant, wearing the royal tiara and armed with a battle-axe. He is shaded by 15 parasols and fanned by legions of servants. The rectangular holes seen in this stretch of relief were created when pieces of the scene containing inscriptions, reputed to possess magical powers, were removed. Near the end of this panel is the rabble-rousing Siamese mercenary army, with their long headdresses, skirts and tridents. Cambo-

THE HEAVENLY MAIDENS

Angkor Wat is famous for its beguiling *apsaras* (heavenly nymphs). There are more than 3000 *apsaras* carved into the walls of Angkor Wat, each of them unique, and there are more than 30 different hairstyles to admire. Many of these exquisite *apsaras* were damaged during Indian efforts to clean the temples with chemicals during the 1980s (the ultimate bad acid trip), but they are now being restored by teams from the **German Apsara Conservation Project** (GACP; www.gacp-angkor.de). The organisation operates a small information booth in the northwest corner of Angkor Wat, near the pagoda, where beautiful black-and-white postcards and images of Angkor are available.

ANGKOR CENTRAL STRUCTURE

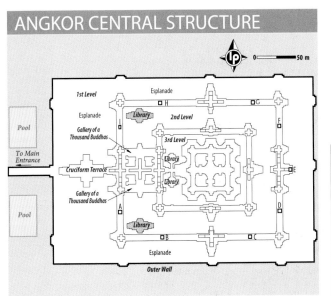

dian tour guides love to point out the contrast between the disciplined Khmer troops, with their square breastplates and spears, and the rather disorderly Siamese.

(C) HEAVEN & HELL

The eastern half of the south gallery depicts the enticing rewards and the gruesome punishments of the 37 heavens and 32 hells. On the left, the upper and middle tiers show people proceeding towards 18-armed Yama (the judge of the dead) seated on a bull. On the lower tier, devils drag the wicked along the road to hell. To Yama's right, the relief is divided into two parts by a line of *garudas* (half-man, half-bird creatures). Above, the chosen dwell in beautiful mansions, served by women and attendants; below, the condemned suffer horrible tortures that aren't so different from Khmer Rouge methods of torture, as seen in Tuol Sleng Prison in Phnom Penh. The lotus-panel ceiling in this section was restored by the French in the 1930s.

(D) CHURNING OF THE OCEAN OF MILK
The southern section of the east gallery is the most famous bas-relief at Angkor Wat, the Churning of the Ocean of Milk. This brilliantly executed carving depicts 88 *asuras* (demons; to the left) and 92 *devas* (gods) with crested helmets, churning up the sea to extract the elixir of immortality. The demons hold the head of a serpent and the gods hold its tail, while the body is coiled around Mt Mandala, which turns and churns the water in this epic tug-of-war. Vishnu, incarnated as a huge turtle, lends his shell to serve as the base and pivot of Mt Mandala. Overhead a host of *apsaras* (heavenly nymphs) sing and dance in encouragement. Luckily for humankind the gods won through, as the *apsaras* above were too much for the hot-blooded demons to take.

(E) ELEPHANT GATE
This gate was used by the king for mounting and dismounting elephants directly from the gallery. North of the gate is a Khmer inscription recording the erection of a nearby stupa in the 18th century.

(F) VISHNU CONQUERS THE DEMONS
The northern section of the east gallery shows a feisty encounter between Vishnu, riding on a *garuda,* and innumerable demons. Needless to say, Vishnu slays all comers. This gallery was completed at a later date, most likely in the 16th century, and the carving is notably more primitive than the original work from the 12th century.

(G) KRISHNA & THE DEMON KING
The eastern section of the north gallery shows Vishnu incarnated as Krishna riding a *garuda*. He flies into the burning residence of Bana, the demon king. The *garuda* puts out the fire and Bana is captured. In the final scene, Krishna kneels before Shiva and asks that Bana's life be spared.

(H) BATTLE OF THE GODS & THE DEMONS
The western section of the north gallery depicts the battle between the 21 gods of the Brahmanic pantheon and various demons. The gods are

featured with their traditional attributes and mounts. Vishnu has four arms and is seated on a *garuda,* while Shiva rides a *hamsa* (sacred goose).

(I) BATTLE OF LANKA

The northern half of the west gallery shows scenes from the *Ramayana*. In the Battle of Lanka, Rama (shown on the shoulders of Hanuman), along with his army of monkeys, battles 10-headed, 20-armed Ravana, seducer of Rama's beautiful wife Sita. Ravana rides on a chariot drawn by monsters and commands an army of giants.

> **VEHICLES OF THE GODS**
> The great Hindu gods still need transport like the rest of us. The vehicle of Vishnu is Garuda, a half-man, half-bird creature who features in many temples and was later combined with his old enemy Naga to promote religious unity under Jayavarman VII. Nandi is the mount of Shiva and there are several statues of Nandi dotted about the temples, although many have been damaged or stolen by looters.

ANGKOR THOM

Aptly named, the fortified city of Angkor Thom is undoubtedly a 'Great City', some 10 sq km in extent. It was built by Angkor's most celebrated king, Jayavarman VII (r 1181–1219), who came to power following the disastrous sacking of the Khmer capital by the Chams. At its height, it may have supported a population of one million people in the surrounding region. Centred on Bayon, Angkor Thom is enclosed by a *jayagiri* (square wall), 8m high and more than 13km in length, and encircled by a 100m-wide *jayasindhu* (moat), said to have been inhabited by fierce crocodiles. This is yet another monumental expression of Mt Meru surrounded by the oceans.

The city has five immense gates, one each in the northern, western and southern walls, and two in the eastern wall. The 20m-high gates are decorated with stone elephant trunks and crowned by four gargantuan faces of the Bodhisattva Avalokiteshvara. In front of the south gate stand giant statues of 54 gods (to the left) and 54 demons (to the right), a motif from the Churning of the Ocean of Milk (see opposite). The south gate is the most popular with visitors, as it has been fully restored and many of the heads (mostly copies) remain in place. However, this gate is on the main road into Angkor Thom from Angkor Wat, and it gets very busy.

ANGKOR THOM

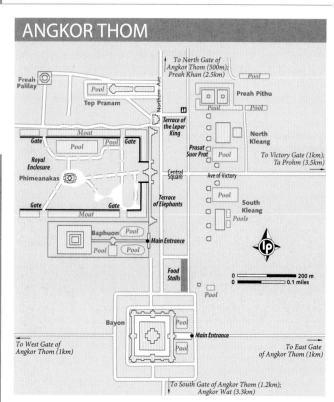

Instead, make for the more peaceful east and west gates, found at the end of uneven trails through the forest. The beautiful east gate was used as a location on *Lara Croft: Tomb Raider,* where the bad guys broke into the 'tomb' by pulling down a giant (polystyrene!) *apsara.* The causeway at the west gate of Angkor Thom has completely collapsed, leaving a jumble of ancient stones sticking out of the soil like victims of a terrible historical pile-up.

In the centre of the walled enclosure are the city's most important monuments, including Bayon, Baphuon, the Royal Enclosure, Phimeanakas and the Terrace of Elephants.

BAYON

Unique Bayon epitomises the creative genius and inflated ego of Cambodia's legendary king, Jayavarman VII. It's a place of stooped corridors, precipitous flights of stairs and a collection of 54 gothic towers decorated with 216 icily smiling, enormous faces of Avalokiteshvara that bear more than a passing resemblance to the great king himself. These huge heads glare down from every angle, exuding power and control with a hint of humanity – precisely the blend required to hold sway over such a vast empire, ensuring the disparate and far-flung population yielded to his magnanimous will. As you walk around, a dozen or more of the heads are visible at any one time – full-face or in profile, almost level with your eyes or staring down from on high.

The enigmatic stone faces of Bayon

THE TEMPLES OF ANGKOR

Though Bayon is now known to have been built by Jayavarman VII, for many years its origins were unknown. Shrouded in dense jungle, it also took researchers some time to realise that it stands at the exact centre of Angkor Thom. There is still much mystery associated with Bayon, but this seems only appropriate for a monument whose signature is the enigmatic smiling face.

The eastward orientation of Bayon leads most people to visit early in the morning, preferably just after sunrise, when the sun inches upwards, lighting face after face.

LAYOUT

Unlike Angkor Wat, which looks impressive from all angles, Bayon looks like a glorified pile of rubble from a distance. Only when you enter the temple and make your way up to the third level does it begin to work its magic.

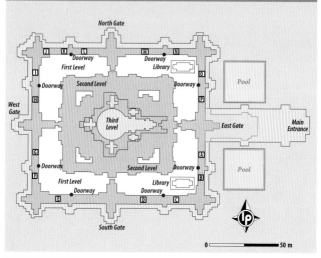

BAYON

The basic structure of Bayon is a simple three levels, which correspond more or less to three distinct building phases. Jayavarman VII began construction of this temple at an advanced age, so was never confident it would be completed. As each phase was finished, he moved on to the next. The first two levels are square and adorned with bas-reliefs. They lead up to a third, circular level, with the towers and their faces.

Some say that the Khmer empire was divided into 54 provinces at the time of Bayon's construction, hence the 54 towers with the all-seeing eyes of Avalokiteshvara (or Jayavarman VII) keeping watch on the kingdom's outlying subjects.

BAS-RELIEFS

Angkor Wat's bas-reliefs might grab the headlines, but those at Bayon are even more extensive, with a total of 1.2km of extraordinary carving featuring more than 11,000 figures. The famous carvings on the outer wall of the first level depict vivid scenes of everyday life around Angkor. The reliefs described in this section are the more intricate carvings on the first level. The sequence assumes that you enter Bayon from the east and view the reliefs in a clockwise direction.

(A) THE CHAMS ON THE RUN

Just south of the east gate is a three-level panorama. On the first tier, Khmer soldiers march off to battle mounted on elephants and ox carts, which are almost exactly like those still used in Cambodia today. The

ON LOCATION WITH TOMB RAIDER

Several sequences for *Lara Croft: Tomb Raider*, starring Angelina Jolie, were shot around the temples of Angkor. The Cambodia shoot opened at Phnom Bakheng with Lara looking through binoculars for the mysterious temple. The baddies were already trying to break in through the east gate of Angkor Thom, by pulling down a giant polystyrene *apsara*. Reunited with her custom Landrover, Lara made a few laps around the Bayon before discovering a back way into the temple from Ta Prohm, where she plucked a sprig of jasmine and fell through into…Pinewood Studios. After battling a living statue and dodging Daniel Craig by diving off the waterfall at Phnom Kulen, she emerged in a floating market in front of Angkor Wat, as you do. She came ashore here before borrowing a mobile phone from a local monk and venturing in to the Gallery of a Thousand Buddhas, where she was healed by the abbot.

second tier depicts the coffins being carried back from the battlefield. In the centre of the third tier, Jayavarman VII, shaded by parasols, is shown on horseback followed closely by legions of concubines.

(B) LINGA WORSHIP
The first panel north of the southeastern corner shows Hindus praying to a *linga* (phallic symbol). This image was probably originally a Buddha, later modified by a Hindu king.

REFRESHMENTS AROUND THE TEMPLES

Water and soft drinks are available throughout the temple area, and many sellers lurk outside the temples, ready to pounce with offers of 'You wanna buy cold drink?' Sometimes they ask at just the right moment; on other occasions it's the 27th time in an hour that you've been approached and you're ready to scream. Try not to – you'll scare your fellow travellers and lose face with the locals.

(C) A NAVAL BATTLE
These exquisitely carved scenes depict a naval battle between the Khmers and the Chams (the latter with head coverings), and everyday life around Tonlé Sap lake, where the battle was fought. Look for images of people picking lice from each other's hair, hunters and, towards the western end of the panel, a woman giving birth.

(D) THE CHAMS VANQUISHED
In the next panel, the scenes from daily life continue and the battle shifts to the shore, where the Chams are soundly thrashed. Scenes include two people playing chess, a cockfight and women selling fish in the market.

(E & F) A MILITARY PROCESSION
The last section of the south gallery, depicting a military procession, is unfinished, as is the panel showing elephants being led down from the mountains. Brahmans have been chased by tigers up two trees.

(G) CIVIL WAR?
This panel depicts scenes that, according to some scholars, depict a civil war. Armed groups confront each other, and the violence escalates until elephants and warriors join the melee.

(H) THE ALL-SEEING KING

The fighting continues on a smaller scale in the next panel. An antelope is being swallowed by a gargantuan fish; among the smaller fish is a prawn, under which an inscription proclaims that the king will seek out those in hiding.

(I) VICTORY PARADE

This panel depicts a procession that includes the king (carrying a bow), and is presumably a celebration of his victory.

(J) THE CIRCUS COMES TO TOWN

At the western corner of the northern wall is a Khmer circus. A strongman holds three dwarfs, and a man on his back is spinning a wheel with his feet; above is a group of tightrope walkers. To the right of the circus, the royal court watches from a terrace, below which is a procession of animals.

Detail of bas-relief, Angkor Thom

(K) A LAND OF PLENTY

The two rivers, one next to the doorpost and the other a few metres to the right, are teeming with fish.

(L, M & N) THE CHAMS RETREAT

On the lowest level of this unfinished three-tiered scene, the Cham armies are being defeated and expelled from the Khmer kingdom. The next panel depicts the Chams advancing, and the badly deteriorated panel shows the Chams (on the left) pursuing the Khmers.

(O) THE CHAMS SACK ANGKOR

This panel shows the war of 1177, when the Khmers were defeated by the Chams and Angkor was pillaged. The wounded Khmer king is being lowered from the back of an elephant and an injured Khmer general is being carried on a hammock suspended from a pole. Directly above, despairing Khmers are getting drunk. The Chams (on the right) are in hot pursuit of their vanquished enemy.

(P) THE CHAMS ENTER ANGKOR

This panel depicts another meeting of the two armies. Notice the flag bearers among the Cham troops (on the right). The Chams were defeated in the war, which ended in 1181, as depicted in panel A.

BAPHUON

Sometimes known as the world's largest jigsaw puzzle, Baphuon was the centre of École Française d'Extrême-Orient (EFEO) restoration efforts when the Cambodian civil war erupted and work stopped for over 20 years. The temple was taken apart piece by piece, in keeping with the anastylosis method of renovation, but all the records were destroyed during the Khmer Rouge years, leaving experts with 300,000 stones to put into place. The EFEO resumed restoration in 1995 and work continues today.

   In its heyday, Baphuon would have been one of the most spectacular of Angkor's temples. Located 200m northwest of Bayon, it's a pyramidal representation of mythical Mt Meru. Construction probably began under Suryavarman I and was later completed by Udayadityavarman II (r 1049–1065). It marked the centre of the capital that existed before the construction of Angkor Thom.

Baphuon is approached by a 200m elevated walkway made of sandstone, and the central structure is 43m high. Clamber under the elevated causeway for an incredible view of the hundreds of pillars supporting it.

On the western side of Baphuon, the retaining wall of the second level was fashioned – apparently in the 15th or 16th century – into a reclining Buddha about 60m in length. The unfinished figure is difficult to make out, but the head is on the northern side of the wall and the gate is where the hips should be; to the left of the gate protrudes an arm. This huge project, undertaken by the Buddhist faithful 500 years ago, reinforces the notion that Angkor was never entirely abandoned.

ROYAL ENCLOSURE & PHIMEANAKAS

Phimeanakas stands close to the centre of a walled area that once housed the royal palace. Phimeanakas means 'Celestial Palace', and some scholars say that it was once topped by a golden spire. Today it only hints at its former splendour, but it's worth clambering up to the upper levels for good views of Baphuon. There's very little left of the royal palace today, as it was constructed of wood (buildings of stone were reserved for the gods). There are two sandstone pools, once the site of royal ablutions, that are now used as swimming holes by local children. The enclosure is fronted to the east by the Terrace of Elephants (p76).

PREAH PALILAY

This Buddhist temple is flanked on all sides by enormous kapok trees that lean inwards like a natural shelter. Preah Palilay is one of the most atmospheric temples around Angkor Thom and is located about 200m north of the Royal Enclosure's northern wall. It was erected during the rule of Jayavarman VII and originally housed a Buddha, which has long since vanished.

TERRACE OF THE LEPER KING

The Terrace of the Leper King, just north of the Terrace of Elephants, is a 7m-high platform. On top of the platform stands a nude, though sexless, statue, another of Angkor's mysteries. Legend has it that at least two of the Angkor kings had leprosy, and the statue may represent one of them. More likely it is Yama, the god of death, and the Terrace of the Leper King probably housed the royal crematorium.

THE TEMPLES OF ANGKOR

Keeping watch over the Terrace of the Leper King, Angkor Thom

The front retaining walls of the terrace are decorated with at least five tiers of meticulously executed carvings of seated *apsaras*. Other figures include kings wearing pointed diadems, accompanied by princesses adorned with beautiful pearls.

On the southern side of the Terrace of the Leper King there is access to the front wall of a hidden terrace that was covered up when the outer structure was built – a terrace within a terrace. The four tiers of *apsaras* and other figures, including *nagas,* look as fresh as if they had been carved yesterday, thanks to being covered up for centuries.

TERRACE OF ELEPHANTS

The 350m-long Terrace of Elephants was a giant viewing stand for public ceremonies and served as a base for the king's grand audience hall. As you stand here, try to imagine the pomp and grandeur of the Khmer empire at its height, with infantry, cavalry, horse-drawn chariots and elephants parading in a colourful procession, pennants and standards aloft. Looking on is the god-king, adorned with a gold crown, shaded by parasols and attended by mandarins and handmaidens. The middle section of the retaining wall is decorated with life-sized *garudas* and lions; towards either end are the two sections of the famous parade of elephants, complete with their Khmer mahouts.

PRASAT SUOR PRAT

The 'Temple of the Tightrope Dancers' consists of 12 laterite towers. Archaeologists believe the towers were constructed by Jayavarman VII and it is likely that each one originally contained either a *linga* or a statue. It is said that artists performed for the king on tightropes or rope-bridges strung between these towers. According to 13th-century Chinese emissary Chou Ta-Kuan, the towers of Suor Prat were also used for public trials of sorts – during a dispute the two parties would be made to sit inside two towers, one party eventually succumbing to disease and proven guilty.

AROUND ANGKOR THOM

PHNOM BAKHENG ✓

Phnom Bakheng is the definitive spot for sunset around Angkor, though the temple itself tends to be forgotten amid the nightly circus. Around 400m south of Angkor Thom, Phnom Bakheng is home to the first of the temple-mountains built in the vicinity of Angkor, and was the centre of Yasodharapura, the new capital of Yasovarman I (r 889–910). The

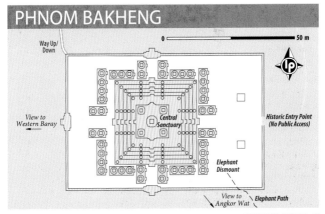

PHNOM BAKHENG

0   50 m

Way Up/
Down

View to
Western Baray

Central
Sanctuary

Historic Entry Point
(No Public Access)

Elephant
Dismount

View to
Angkor Wat

Elephant Path

THE LONG STRIDER

One of Vishnu's best-loved incarnations was when he appeared as the dwarf Vamana, and proceeded to reclaim the world from the evil demon-king Bali. The dwarf politely asked the demon-king for a comfortable patch of ground upon which to meditate, saying that the patch need only be big enough so that he could easily walk across it in three paces. The demon-king agreed, only to see the dwarf swell into a mighty giant who strode across the universe in three enormous steps. From this legend, Vishnu is sometimes known as 'the long strider'.

temple-mountain has five tiers, with seven levels (including the base and the summit) representing the seven Hindu heavens.

Visit at sunset and you may have to share it with all the other tourists at Angkor. Some prefer to visit in the early morning, when it is cool to climb the hill and the crowds are light. That said, the sunset over the Western Baray is very impressive from here.

It is possible to ascend the hill by elephant (US$15 per person one way), and the location certainly makes for a memorable approach. Some people aren't comfortable with the idea of elephants hauling themselves up the hill, but they are extremely well looked after. It's advisable to book in advance, as the rides are very popular with tour groups.

The main steep approach to Phnom Bakheng is currently closed and it is necessary to follow a winding path to the right, taking about 20 minutes to the summit.

PRASAT KRAVAN

It's uninspiring from the outside, but the brick carvings concealed within its towers are Prasat Kravan's hidden treasures. The five brick towers, arranged in a north–south line and oriented to the east, were built for Hindu worship in 921.

Prasat Kravan was partially restored in 1968, returning the carvings to their former glory. The largest, central tower has images of Vishnu: showing him as an eight-armed deity on the back wall; taking the three gigantic steps with which he reclaimed the world on the left wall; and riding a *garuda* on the right wall. The northernmost tower displays bas-reliefs of Vishnu's consort, Lakshmi.

Prasat Kravan is about 2km east of Angkor Wat.

BANTEAY KDEI & SRA SRANG

North of Prasat Kravan, Banteay Kdei is a massive Buddhist monastery from the latter part of the 12th century, surrounded by four concentric walls. Each of its four entrances is decorated with *garudas,* which hold aloft the four faces of Avalokiteshvara. The inside of the central tower was never finished and much of the temple is in a ruinous state due to its hasty construction.

Just east of Banteay Kdei is a basin of earlier construction, Sra Srang (Pool of Ablutions), measuring 800m by 400m. It was reserved for the king and his wives. A tiny island in the middle once bore a wooden temple, of which only the stone base remains. This is a beautiful body of water from which to take in a quiet sunrise or sunset.

TA PROHM ✓

The ultimate Indiana Jones fantasy, Ta Prohm is cloaked in dappled shadow, its crumbling towers and walls locked in the slow, muscular embrace of vast root systems. If Angkor Wat, Bayon and other temples are testimony to the genius of the ancient Khmers, Ta Prohm reminds

Nature reconquers at Ta Prohm

us equally of the awesome fecundity and power of the jungle. There is a poetic cycle to this venerable ruin, with humanity first conquering nature to rapidly create, and nature once again conquering humanity to slowly destroy.

Undoubtedly the most atmospheric ruin at Angkor, Ta Prohm has been left to be swallowed by the jungle, and looks very much the way most of the monuments of Angkor appeared when European explorers first stumbled upon them. Well, that's the theory, but in fact the jungle is groomed and only the largest trees are left in place, making it a controlled ruin rather than a raw one like Beng Mealea (p99). Still, a visit to Ta Prohm is a unique, otherworldly experience.

Built from 1186 and originally known as Rajavihara (Monastery of the King), Ta Prohm was a Buddhist temple dedicated to the mother of Jayavarman VII. It is one of the few temples in the Angkor region where an inscription provides information about the temple's dependents

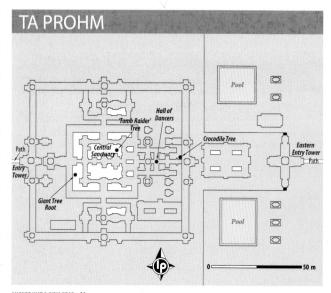

TA PROHM

Nhiem Chun
The sweeper of Ta Prohm (p79) from 1941 to 2005

What was your job at Ta Prohm? There is a battle between nature and man at the temple. I had to sweep, as otherwise the leaves would cover the temple. **How do you feel about Ta Prohm?** These temples are the spirit of the Cambodian nation. I could have built this temple in a past life. If I did not have any connection, I would not be here to take care of it today. **You became very famous when you graced the cover of the 4th edition of Lonely Planet's Cambodia.** Yes, many tourists wanted their photo taken with me and I sold small trinkets to supplement my income. **What will happen to the temples of Angkor in the future?** I am old now. I can't take care of these temples any more. But when I am gone, these stones will still be here. These temples are the symbols of our soul. We will not survive if we don't look after our temples.

and inhabitants. Apparently, close to 80,000 people were required to maintain or attend at the temple, among them more than 2700 officials and 615 dancers.

Ta Prohm is a temple of towers, enclosed courtyards and narrow corridors. Many of the corridors are impassable, clogged with jumbled piles of delicately carved stone blocks dislodged by the roots of long-decayed trees. Bas-reliefs on bulging walls are carpeted with lichen, moss and creeper. Ancient trees tower overhead, their leaves filtering the sunlight and casting a greenish pall over the whole scene. The most popular of the many strangulating root formations is the 'crocodile tree', on the inside of the easternmost *gopura* (entrance pavilion) of the central enclosure.

TA KEO

North of Ta Prohm, Ta Keo is a stark, undecorated temple that undoubtedly would have been one of the finest of Angkor's structures, had it

The unfinished Ta Keo temple

LET'S TALK ABOUT SEX

Fertility symbols are prominent around the temples of Angkor. The *linga* is a phallic symbol and would have originally been located within the towers of most Hindu temples. It sits inside a *yoni*, the female fertility symbol, combining to produce holy water, charged with the sexual energy of creation. Brahmans poured water over the *linga*; it drained through the *yoni* and out of the temples through elaborate gutters, to anoint the pilgrims outside.

been finished. Built by Jayavarman V (r 968–1001), it was dedicated to Shiva and was the first Angkorian monument built entirely of sandstone. The summit of the central tower, which is surrounded by four lower towers, is almost 50m high.

No-one is certain why work was never completed at Ta Keo, but a likely cause may have been the death of Jayavarman V. According to inscriptions, Ta Keo was struck by lightning during construction, which may have been a bad omen and led to its abandonment. Others suggest it may have been down to the high-quality sandstone, which was simply too hard to carve.

SPEAN THMOR

Spean Thmor (Stone Bridge), of which an arch and several piers remain, is northwest of Ta Keo. Jayavarman VII, the last great builder of Angkor, constructed many roads with these immense stone bridges spanning watercourses, but this is the only large bridge remaining in the immediate vicinity of Angkor. There's an impressive 19-arched bridge, Spean Praptos, in Kompong Kdei, about 65km southeast of Siem Reap on the road to Phnom Penh.

PREAH KHAN

One of the largest complexes at Angkor, Preah Khan (Sacred Sword) is a maze of vaulted corridors, fine carvings and lichen-clad stonework. It was built by Jayavarman VII and probably served as his temporary residence while Angkor Thom was under construction. Like Ta Prohm, it is a place of towered enclosures and shoulder-hugging corridors. Unlike Ta Prohm, however, the temple of Preah Khan is in a good state of preservation thanks to the ongoing restoration efforts of the **World Monuments Fund** (WMF; www.wmf.org).

The central sanctuary of the temple was dedicated in 1191 and a large stone stele tells us much about Preah Khan's role as a centre for worship and learning. The temple was dedicated to 515 divinities, and during the course of a year 18 major festivals took place here, requiring a team of thousands to maintain the place.

Preah Khan covers a very large area, but the temple itself is contained within a rectangular enclosing wall of around 500m by 600m. Four processional walkways approach the gates of the temple, and these are bordered by another stunning depiction of the Churning of the Ocean of Milk – as seen at Angkor Thom – although most of the heads have disappeared (presently only the west side remains in reasonable condition).

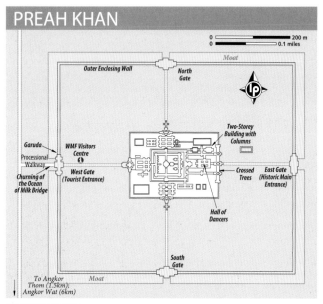

From the central sanctuary, four long, vaulted galleries extend in the cardinal directions. Many of the interior walls of Preah Khan were once coated with plaster that was held in place by holes in the stone. Today many delicate carvings remain, including *essais* (wise men) and *apsaras*.

As with most of the other Angkorian temples, the main entrance to Preah Khan is in the east. However, most tourists enter at the west gate near the main road, then walk the length of the temple to the east gate before doubling back to the central sanctuary and exiting at the north gate. This is reason enough to rip up the rule book and enter from the original entrance in the east. Look out for the curious Grecian-style two-storey structure on the eastern side of the temple: its purpose is unknown, but it looks like an exile from Athens.

Preah Khan is a genuine fusion temple. Its eastern entrance is dedicated to Mahayana Buddhism, and features equal-sized doors; the other cardinal directions are dedicated to Shiva, Vishnu and Brahma, with successively smaller doors emphasising the unequal nature of Hinduism.

> **UNRAVELLING THE NAGA**
> The *naga* is one of the most prominent symbols of Khmer mythology. The multi-headed serpent is the half-brother and enemy of the *garuda* and is frequently seen on causeways, doorways and roofs. The *naga* controls water and the rains, and therefore the prosperity of the kingdom. The seven-headed *naga*, a feature of many temples, represents the rainbow that acts as a bridge between heaven and earth.

PREAH NEAK POAN

An island temple to the east of Preah Khan, Preah Neak Poan (Intertwined Serpents) is believed to celebrate Buddha's achievement of nirvana. Dating from the late-12th century, this Buddhist temple is petite yet perfect and was constructed by (yes, it's him again) Jayavarman VII. It has a large, square pool surrounded by four smaller square pools. In the centre of the main pool is a circular 'island' encircled by the two *nagas* whose intertwined tails give the temple its name. The four fountains of the smaller pools take the forms of elephant, human, lion and horse heads, and originally spouted holy water that could cure pilgrims of their ailments.

PREAH NEAK POAN

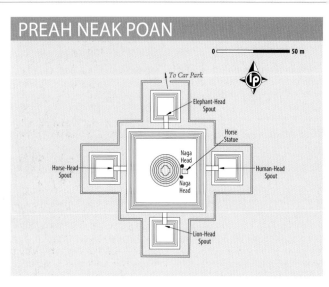

Although it has been centuries since the small pools were last filled with water, it's a safe bet that when the Encore Angkor casino is inevitably developed in Las Vegas, Preah Neak Poan will provide the blueprint for the ultimate swimming complex.

Preah Neak Poan was originally in the centre of a huge 3km-by-900m *baray* (reservoir) serving Preah Khan. Known as Jayatataka, it's now dried up and overgrown.

TA SOM

East of Preah Neak Poan, Ta Som is yet another of the late-12th-century Buddhist temples of Jayavarman VII, the Donald Trump of ancient Cambodia. The central area is in a ruinous state, but restoration by the WMF is close to completion. The most impressive feature at Ta Som is the huge strangler fig completely overwhelming the eastern *gopura*, providing one of the most iconic photo opportunities in the Angkor area.

EASTERN BARAY & EASTERN MEBON

An enormous reservoir, the Eastern Baray was excavated by Yaso-varman I, who marked its four corners with steles. This basin, now entirely dried up, measured 7km by 1.8km and was originally fed by the Siem Reap River.

The Hindu temple known as the Eastern Mebon, erected by Rajen-dravarman II (r 944–968), would have originally been on an island in the centre of the Eastern Baray. Its temple-mountain form is topped off by the now-familiar quincuncial arrangement of towers. The elaborate brick shrines are dotted with neatly arranged holes, which attached the original plasterwork.

The base of the temple is guarded at its corners by perfectly carved stone figures of elephants. The Eastern Mebon is flanked by earthen ramps, a clue that this temple was never finished, and a good visual guide as to how the temples were constructed.

PRE RUP

Pre Rup, built by Rajendravarman II, is about 1km south of the Eastern Mebon. Like its nearby predecessor, it consists of a pyramid-shaped temple-mountain with the uppermost of the three tiers supporting five lotus towers. The brick sanctuaries were also once decorated with a plaster coating, fragments of which still remain on the southwestern tower. Several of the outermost eastern towers are perilously close to collapse and are propped up by an army of wooden supports.

Pre Rup means 'Turning the Body' and refers to a traditional method of cremation in which a corpse's outline is traced in the cinders, first in one direction and then in the other. This suggests that the temple may have served as an early royal crematorium.

WHEN NATURE CALLS

Angkor is now blessed with some of the finest public toilets in Asia. Housed in wooden chalets, they wouldn't be out of place in a fancy hotel. The trouble is that the guardians often choose not to run the generators that power the toilets, meaning they can be pretty dark.

Remember, in remote areas, don't stray off the path – being seen in a compromising position is infinitely better than stepping on a land mine.

THE TEMPLES OF ANGKOR

Pre Rup is one of the most popular sunset spots around Angkor, as the view over the surrounding rice fields of the Eastern Baray is beautiful.

BANTEAY SAMRÉ

Banteay Samré dates from the same period as Angkor Wat and was built by Suryavarman II. The temple is in a fairly healthy state of preservation due to some extensive renovation work. The area consists of a central temple with four wings, preceded by a hall and two libraries, the southern one remarkably well preserved. The whole ensemble is enclosed by two large concentric walls around what would have been the unique feature of an inner moat, now dried up.

Handicrafts on sale at Pre Rup (p87)

Banteay Samré is 400m east of the Eastern Baray. Follow the road to the village of Preah Dak and continue straight ahead rather than turning to the left towards Banteay Srei. A visit here can be combined with a trip to Banteay Srei.

WESTERN BARAY & WESTERN MEBON

The Western Baray, measuring an incredible 8km by 2.3km, was constructed by hand to provide water for the intensive cultivation of lands around Angkor. Just for the record, these enormous *baray* weren't dug out, but were created by building up huge dykes around the edges. In the centre of the Western Baray is the ruin of the Western Mebon temple, where a giant bronze statue of Vishnu, now in the National Museum in Phnom Penh, was found. The Western Mebon is accessible by boat from the dam on the southern shore.

WALKING TOUR

TREKKING AROUND ANGKOR THOM

Spread over a vast area of the steamy tropical lowlands of Cambodia, the temples of Angkor aren't the ideal candidates to tackle on foot. However, the area is blanketed in mature forest, offering plenty of shade, and following back roads into temples is the perfect way to leave behind the crowds.

Angkor Thom is the top trekking spot, thanks to its manageable size and the number of rewarding temples within its walls. Starting out at the spectacular **south gate** (**1**; p67), admire the immense representation of the Churning of the Ocean of Milk before bidding farewell to the masses and their motorised transport. Ascend the wall of this ancient city and head west, with views of the vast moat to the left and the thick jungle to the right. It's often possible to see forest birds along this route, as it is very peaceful. Reaching the southwest corner, admire **Prasat Chrung** (**2**), one of four identical temples marking the corners of the city. Head down below to see the drainage channels of this once-powerful city, which was crisscrossed by canals in its heyday.

Back on the gargantuan wall, continue to the **west gate** (**3**; p68), looking out for a view to the immense Western Baray on your left. Descend at the west gate and admire the artistry of its incredible central tower. Wander east along the path into the heart of Angkor Thom, but don't be diverted by the beauty of Bayon, as this is best saved until last.

Veer north into **Baphuon** (**4**; p74) and wander to the back of what some have called the 'world's largest jigsaw puzzle'. Pass

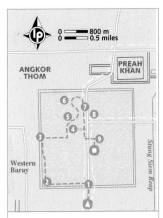

distance 7km **duration** about five hours, including temple visits ▶ **start** south gate of Angkor Thom ● **end** Bayon through the small temple of **Phimeanakas** (**5**; p75) and the former royal palace compound, an area of towering trees, tumbling walls and atmospheric foliage. Continue further north to petite but pretty **Preah Palilay** (**6**; p75), guarded by giant kapok trees.

It's time to make for the mainstream with a walk through the **Terrace of the Leper King** (**7**; p75) and along the front of the royal viewing gallery, the Terrace of Elephants. If there is time, you may want to zigzag east to visit the laterite towers of **Prasat Suor Prat** (**8**; p77); otherwise continue to the top billing of **Bayon** (**9**; p69). Weird yet wonderful, this is one of most enigmatic of the temples at Angkor. Take your time to decipher the bas-reliefs before venturing up to the legendary faces on the upper level.

Gambling, Cambodian style

EXCURSIONS

PREK TOAL BIRD SANCTUARY

Prek Toal is one of three biospheres on Tonlé Sap lake, and the incredible bird sanctuary makes it the most worthwhile and straightforward to visit. It is an ornithologist's fantasy come true, with a significant number of rare breeds gathered in one small area, including the lesser and greater adjutant storks, the milky stork and the spot-billed pelican. Even the uninitiated will be impressed, as these birds have huge wingspans and build enormous nests.

Visitors during the dry season (December to May) will find the concentration of birds like something out of a Hitchcock film. As water starts to dry up elsewhere, the birds congregate here. Serious twitchers know that the best time to see birds is early morning or late afternoon, and this means an early start or an overnight at Prek Toal's environment office, where there are basic beds for US$7. For real enthusiasts, it may be best to head out of Siem Reap after lunch, to get to the sanctuary at around 4pm for an afternoon viewing. Stay overnight and view the birds in the morning before returning to town.

Osmose, a nonprofit company in Siem Reap, offers organised tours to help promote responsible tourism in Cambodia and contributes to the conservation of the area. Day trips include transportation (with hotel pick-up), entrance fees, guides, breakfast, lunch and water. Osmose can also arrange overnight trips for serious enthusiasts. Proceeds go towards educating children and villagers about the importance of the birds and

INFORMATION

Location About 40km southwest of Siem Reap.
Getting there Getting to the sanctuary under your own steam involves a 20-minute *moto* (US$4) or taxi (US$15) to Chong Kneas, and then a boat to the environment office (around US$40 return, one hour each way). From here, a small boat (US$20 including a guide) will take you into the sanctuary, about one hour beyond.
Contact Osmose (☎ 012 832812; www.osmosetonlesap.net)
Costs US$80 per person for a day trip with Osmose.
When to go Osmose trips start at 6am and finish at 6pm, including transfers, but serious twitchers should consider undertaking an overnight trip. December to March is the ideal time to visit.

the unique flooded forest environment; the day trip includes the chance to visit one of the local communities.

Binoculars are available at Prek Toal for those who don't carry their own. Sunscreen and head protection are essential, as it can get very hot in the dry season. The guides at the environment office are equipped with booklets with the bird names in English, but they speak little English themselves, hence the advantage of travelling with Osmose.

FLOATING VILLAGE OF CHONG KNEAS

This famous floating village is extremely popular with visitors wanting a break from the temples, and is an easy excursion to arrange independently. Visitors travelling to or from Phnom Penh by fast boat get a preview, as the floating village is near Phnom Krom, where the boat docks. It is very scenic in the warm light of early morning or late afternoon and can be combined with a view of the sunset from the hilltop temple of

Daily bustle in the floating village of Chong Kneas

INFORMATION

Location Between 11km and 15km from Siem Reap, depending on the level of Tonlé Sap lake.
Getting there From Siem Reap, a round-trip costs about US$4 by *moto*, US$6 by *remorque-moto* and US$15 by taxi. The trip takes 20 minutes one-way.
Costs A local cooperative has fixed boat prices at US$10 per person. On top of this, there are charges for road use and security, so you'll end up paying around US$12 or US$13, although there are rumours of a hike to US$20.
When to go Chong Kneas can be visited at any time during daylight hours, but it tends to be quieter earlier in the morning.

Phnom Krom. The downside is that tour groups tend to take over, and boats end up chugging up and down the channels in convoy.

The village moves depending on the season and you need to rent a boat to explore properly. Visitors should also check out the **Gecko Centre** (www.tsbr-ed.org; 🕑 8.30am-5.30pm), an informative place located in the floating village. It has displays on flora and fauna of the area, as well as information on communities living around the lake.

KOMPONG PHHLUK

Kompong Phhluk is an incredible village of bamboo skyscrapers that rise from the lakeshore like a set from *Waterworld*. More memorable than Chong Kneas, but harder to reach, this is an otherworldly place where all the houses are built on soaring stilts about 6m or 7m high. A visit during the wet season is most rewarding, as the water laps at the wooden supports, and pigs, chickens and even crocodiles bob about in floating pens. It may be possible to spot a sky burial in the nearby trees, as some communities still embalm dead bodies while awaiting dry wood, and dry land, for cremation.

INFORMATION

Location About 25km southeast of Siem Reap.
Getting there There are two ways to get to Kompong Phhluk: one is via the floating village of Chong Kneas, where a boat (US$30, one hour) can be arranged; the other is via the small town of Roluos, by a combination of road and boat (US$15).
When to go Kompong Phhluk can be visited at any time of day, but it is best to avoid the heat.

Pich Kran
Fisherman on Tonlé Sap lake

When did you first start fishing? It was back in 1981, when I followed my father into the family trade. **What is the best time of year for fishing?** Usually November and December, when the lake is full of fish and the weather gentle. We don't fish from June to October, the spawning season, to give the stocks a chance to recover. **What is the average catch on the lake?** Working with my team of up to 20 colleagues, we usually catch about seven tonnes of fish a week in the lake. **What is the most lucrative fish to catch?** I would say *trey chadao*, a big fish with succulent meat. What is the tastiest fish? Either *trey keh* or *trey chaow*. **Do you expect your children to continue the family trade?** No, I don't want them to become fishermen, as it such a hard life. There are more opportunities these days.

THE HEARTBEAT OF CAMBODIA

Tonlé Sap is the largest freshwater lake in Southeast Asia, an incredible natural phenomenon that provides fish proteins and irrigation waters for almost half the population of Cambodia.

The lake is linked to the Mekong at Phnom Penh by a 100km-long channel, known as the Tonlé Sap river. During the wet season, from mid-May to early October, the level of the Mekong rises rapidly, forcing the Tonlé Sap river to reverse its flow into the Tonlé Sap lake. During this period, the lake swells from 2500 sq km to 13,000 sq km or more, its maximum depth increasing from about 2.2m to more than 10m. Around the start of October, as the level of the Mekong begins to fall, the river reverses again, draining the waters of the lake back into the Mekong.

This extraordinary process makes Tonlé Sap lake one of the world's richest sources of freshwater fish. The fishing industry supports about one million people in Cambodia and an individual's catch on the great lake can average 100kg to 200kg per day in the dry season. Worryingly, stocks have dwindled in recent years, partly due to overfishing and partly due to environmental pressures such as upstream dams that affect migration patterns.

To the south, the village is hemmed in by flooded forest that is inundated every year when the lake rises to take the Mekong's overflow. As the lake drops the petrified trees are revealed. Exploring this area by wooden dugout in the wet season is very atmospheric.

THE TEMPLES OF ROLUOS

The monuments of Roluos, which served as Indravarman I's (r 877–889) capital, Hariharalaya, are among the earliest major temple complexes built by the Khmers and mark the dawn of classical art at Angkor. There are contemporary Buddhist monasteries at both Bakong and Lolei.

For those staying in Siem Reap, consider a visit to the nearby market town of Roluos to experience a slice of real Cambodian life. Located along a shady riverbank, the local market is a world away from the tourist mecca of Siem Reap. The town lies just a few kilometres east of Bakong.

PREAH KO

Preah Ko was built by Indravarman I in 880, and was dedicated to Shiva. The six *prasat* (stone halls), aligned in two rows and decorated with carved sandstone and plaster reliefs, face east. Preah Ko has some of the best surviving examples of plasterwork seen at Angkor and is currently under restoration by a German team. There are elaborate inscriptions in the ancient Hindu language of Sanskrit on the door frames of each tower.

The towers of Preah Ko, which means 'Sacred Ox', feature three *nandi* (sacred oxen), all of whom look like a few steaks have been sliced off them over the years.

BAKONG

Bakong is the largest and most striking of the temples at Roluos. Also built by Indravarman I and dedicated to Shiva, it is a representation of Mt Meru. The east-facing complex consists of a five-tier central pyramid of sandstone, 60m square at the base, flanked by eight towers of brick and sandstone.

The complex is enclosed by three concentric walls and a vast moat. There are well-preserved statues of stone elephants on each corner of the first three levels of the central temple. The sanctuary on the fifth level was a later embellishment during the reign of Suryavarman II, in the style of Angkor Wat's central tower.

INFORMATION

Location The temples are 13km east of Siem Reap along NH6. Preah Ko is 600m south of NH6, Bakong 1.5km south and Lolei about 400m north.

Getting there Whatever your favoured means of getting around Angkor – car, *remorque-moto, moto,* bicycle – it will also do the trick for Roluos. Cyclists should consider the country back roads that fan out from the Wat Dam Nak area of Siem Reap.

Costs Entry is included in the general Angkor ticket.

When to go Roluos is open from dawn until dusk, but skip mid-morning or mid-afternoon to avoid the crowds.

LOLEI

The four brick towers of Lolei, which owe much to the design of Preah Ko, were built on an island in the centre of the Indratataka *baray* (reservoir) by Yasovarman I (r 889–910), the founder of the first city at Angkor. According to one of the inscriptions, the four towers were dedicated by Yasovarman I to his mother, his father and his maternal grandparents on 12 July 893.

BANTEAY SREI

Banteay Srei is considered by many to be the jewel in the crown of Angkorian art. A Hindu temple dedicated to Shiva, it is cut from stone of a pinkish hue and includes some of the finest carvings seen anywhere on earth. One of the smallest sites at Angkor, what it lacks in size it makes up for in stature. Banteay Srei means 'Citadel of the Women' and it is said that it must have been built by a woman, as the elaborate carvings are considered too fine for the hand of a man.

Construction on Banteay Srei began in 967 and it is one of the few temples around Angkor not to be commissioned by a king, but by a Brahman. The temple is square and has entrances at the east and west, the east approached by a causeway. Classic carvings at Banteay Srei include delicate women with lotus flowers clearly visible in their hands, as well as breathtaking re-creations of scenes from the epic *Ramayana* adorning

Detail from bas-relief, Banteay Srei

the library pediments. Almost every inch of the interior buildings are covered in decoration.

Banteay Srei was the first major temple restoration undertaken by the École Française d'Extrême-Orient (EFEO) in 1930 using the anastylosis method. The project was a major success and soon led to larger projects. However, it was not the first time the temple had hit the headlines: in 1923 Frenchman André Malraux was arrested for attempting to steal several of the site's major statues.

When Banteay Srei was first rediscovered, it was assumed to be from the 13th or 14th century, as the refined carving must have come at the end of the Angkor period. It was later dated to 967, from inscriptions found at the site. However some scholars are calling for a revision of this date, given that the style of this temple is unlike anything else seen in the 10th century. New theories suggest that, like the great cathedrals of Europe, some Angkorian temples may have been destroyed and then rebuilt, or altered beyond recognition.

BENG MEALEA

Beng Mealea is a spectacular sight to behold. It's one of the most mysterious temples at Angkor, as nature has well and truly run riot here: exploring this *Titanic* of temples is Angkor's ultimate lost-temple experience.

Built in the 12th century under Suryavarman II (r 1112–1152), to the same floorplan as Angkor Wat, Beng Mealea is enclosed by a massive moat measuring 1.2km by 900m, much of which has dried up today. The temple is at the centre of an ancient Angkorian road connecting Angkor Thom and Preah Khan in Preah Vihear Province.

Beng Mealea used to be utterly subsumed by jungle, but some of the dense foliage has been cut back in recent years. Entering from the south, visitors wend their way over piles of masonry, through long dark chambers and between hanging vines to arrive at the central tower, which has completely collapsed. Hidden away among the rubble and foliage are several impressive carvings, and a well-preserved library in the northeastern quadrant. There is also a large wooden walkway to the centre, originally constructed for the filming of Jean-Jacques Annaud's *Two Brothers* (2004).

The temple is a special place and it is worth taking the time to explore thoroughly.

Walkway through the ruins, Beng Mealea

INFORMATION

Location Beng Mealea is about 40km east of Bayon (as the crow flies) and 6.5km southeast of Phnom Kulen. By road it's about 70km (an hour or so) from Siem Reap.

Getting there Travel via the town of Dam Dek, located on NH6 towards Phnom Penh. Turn north immediately after the market and continue on this road for about 35km. The entrance to the temple lies just beyond the left-hand turn to Koh Ker. This is a private road: it usually costs US$2.50 each way for a car, US$1 for a motorbike.

Costs Beng Mealea is not included in the Angkor ticket; it costs US$5 to visit.

When to go Lunchtime is very quiet, plus it's cool and shady thanks to the jungle cover. Otherwise consider the afternoon, as most groups seem to visit in the morning. It's possible to undertake a long day-trip combining Beng Mealea with Kbal Spean and Banteay Srei.

KBAL SPEAN

Kbal Spean is a spectacularly carved riverbed, set deep in the jungle to the northeast of Angkor. Commonly referred to in English as the River of a Thousand Lingas, its name actually means 'bridgehead', a reference to the natural rock bridge at the site. *Lingas* (phallic symbols) have been elaborately carved into the riverbed, and images of Hindu deities are dotted about the area. Kbal Spean was 'discovered' in 1969, when EFEO ethnologist Jean Boulbet was shown the area by an *essai* (wise man). The area was soon off-limits due to the civil war, only becoming safe again in 1998.

It's a 2km uphill walk to the carvings, so carry plenty of water as there is none available at the summit. It's best to start with the river carvings and work back down to the waterfall to cool off, but visitors between January and June will be disappointed to see very little water here.

Nearby is the **Angkor Centre for Conservation of Biodiversity** (www.accb-cambodia .org), committed to rescuing, rehabilitating and reintroducing threatened wildlife. Tours of the centre can be arranged daily at 1pm.

PHNOM KULEN

Phnom Kulen is considered by Khmers to be the most sacred mountain in Cambodia and is a popular place of pilgrimage during weekends and festivals. It played a significant role in the history of the Khmer empire, as it was from here in 802 that Jayavarman II proclaimed himself a *devaraja* (god-king), giving birth to modern-day Cambodia.

EXCURSIONS

There is a small wat located at the summit of the mountain, which houses a large **reclining Buddha** carved into the sandstone boulder upon which it is built. The views from the 487m peak are tremendous, as you can see right across the forested plateau. Nearby is a large **waterfall** and above it are smaller bathing areas and a number of carvings in the riverbed, including numerous *lingas*. Near the top of the waterfall is a jungle-clad temple known as **Prasat Krau Romeas**, dating from the 9th century.

KOH KER

Abandoned to the forests of the north for centuries, Koh Ker, capital of the Angkorian empire from 928 to 944, was long one of Cambodia's most remote and inaccessible temple complexes. However, the opening of a toll road from Dam Dek (via Beng Mealea) puts Koh Ker within day-tripping distance of Siem Reap.

Most visitors start at **Prasat Krahom** (Red Temple), named for the red bricks from which it is constructed. Sadly, none of the carved lions for which this temple was once known remain, although there's still plenty to see – stone archways and galleries lean hither and thither, and impressive stone carvings grace lintels, doorposts and slender window columns. A *naga* (serpent)-flanked causeway and series of sanctuaries, libraries and gates lead past trees and vegetation-covered ponds. Just west of Prasat Krahom, at the far end of a half-fallen colonnade, are the remains of an impressive statue of Nandi.

Jumping for joy at Koh Ker

EXCURSIONS

The principal monument at Koh Ker is **Prasat Thom** (Prasat Kompeng), a 55m-wide, 40m-high sandstone-faced pyramid with seven tiers. This striking structure, which almost looks more Mayan than Khmer, offers spectacular views across the forest from its summit. Look out for the giant *garudas* (half-man, half-bird creatures) under the collapsed chamber at the top of the vertigo-inducing stairs. Some 40 inscriptions, dating from 932 to 1010, have been found at Prasat Thom.

South of the central group is a *baray* (reservoir), measuring 1185m by 548m, known as the **Rahal**. It is fed by the Sen River, which supplied water to irrigate the land in this arid area.

Some of the largest *lingas* in Cambodia can still be seen in a cluster of four temples about 1km northeast of Prasat Thom. The largest is in **Prasat Thneng**, and **Prasat Leung** is similarly well endowed. We're talking breadth rather than length!

Other interesting temples include **Prasat Bram** (the first you come to after passing the toll booths), which is named in honour of its five towers, two of which are smothered by strangler figs; **Prasat Neang Khmau**, with some fine lintels decorating its otherwise bland exterior; and **Prasat Chen**,

DANGER: MINES!

There are no land mines around the main Angkor area. However, visitors venturing further afield to Phnom Kulen and Koh Ker must always stick to marked paths, as there are mines in the vicinity. Visit the Cambodia Land Mine Museum (p50) to learn more about these enemies within.

INFORMATION

Location Koh Ker is 127km northeast of Siem Reap (two hours or so by car) and the road is now pretty much paved all the way, making for a smooth ride.

Getting there Koh Ker is a little too far to consider travelling by *moto* or *remorque-moto*. Hire a car with driver for about US$60 for the day, including a stop at Beng Mealea. Pick-up trucks run from Siem Reap to Srayong, about 9km from Koh Ker, and fares start from 10,000r on the back. Negotiate with a *moto* driver in Srayong for a tour of Koh Ker; expect to pay about US$5 for a half-day.

Costs Entry is not included in the Angkor ticket; it costs US$10 per person.

When to go It's a full-day trip, so you're looking at leaving in the morning and returning late afternoon. Road conditions can be more difficult in the wet season, but the countryside is lush and green.

where a statue of wrestling monkeys (now in the National Museum in Phnom Penh) was discovered.

Koh Ker is one of the least-studied temple areas from the Angkorian period. Louis Delaporte visited in 1880 during his extensive investigations into Angkorian temples. It was surveyed in 1921 by the great Henri Parmentier, but no restoration work was ever undertaken here. Archaeological surveys were carried out by Cambodian teams in the 1950s and 1960s, but all records vanished during the 1970s, helping to preserve this complex as something of an enigma.

For information on preservation and sustainable development plans for Koh Ker, see the website of **Heritage Watch** (www.heritagewatch.org).

Siem Reap is the life-support system for the temples of Angkor, the world's finest collection of religious monuments. Catch the best of the temple action and unravel the myths and legends that adorn their walls before retiring to Siem Reap, the base for a stylish stay complete with feisty flavours, designer drinks and slick spas.

One-stop shop – hair, nails and naps, Siem Reap

ACCOMMODATION

Siem Reap has the best range of accommodation in Cambodia. Whatever your budget, no matter how refined your taste, there will be something that suits. Historic hotels, romantic retreats, boutique hideaways, traditional teak homes, family-run guesthouses and budget crashpads – they are all here.

For the best of the midrange and top-end places, it's essential to book ahead from November to March. Competition in this sector can be fierce, meaning some tempting low-season discounts. Booking online or through a travel agent can save considerably on the walk-in rate.

Those planning for life at the top face a teasing choice of ultra-exclusive resorts, boutique spa stays and international chain hotels with a tad more character than those of the average Asian city. Rates run from US$100 to US$1000, more if life is suite. Most of these hotels levy an additional 10% government tax, 2% tourist tax and sometimes 10% for service, but breakfast is included.

The best deals in Siem Reap come in the midrange bracket, where atmosphere, ambience and comfort combine at prices that are simply a steal compared to the West. Anyone intent on rest and relaxation can head out of town to plush properties set in lush gardens; night owls can stay in the thick of the action. Rates for midrange properties run from about US$25 to US$100 and usually include breakfast, plus a free arrival transfer from the airport or boat dock.

Guesthouses and mini-hotels have been sprouting like mushrooms to cater for backpackers. Most family-run guesthouses charge US$3 to

Need a place to stay? Find and book it at lonelyplanet.com. More than 20 properties are featured for Siem Reap – each personally visited, thoroughly reviewed and happily recommended by a Lonely Planet author. From hostels to high-end hotels, we've hunted out the places that will bring you unique and special experiences. Read independent reviews by authors and other travellers, and get practical information including amenities, maps and photos. Then reserve your room simply and securely via Hotels & Hostels – our online booking service. It's all at lonelyplanet.com/hotels.

US$15 a room, while upmarket guesthouses and small hotels start from US$20 per room, but may include a small pool. Touts for budget guest-houses wait at the bus station, boat dock and airport, offering a free ride into town if you take a room.

When it comes to choosing a location, certain areas have distinct per-sonalities. The central areas around Psar Chaa (Old Market) and Sivatha St are perfect for browsing restaurants and bars, but it can get a little noisy by night, depending on how close you are to Bar St.

The riverside remains a rewarding area and a good hunting ground for midrangers. East of the river towards Wat Bo, the backstreets offer a good combination of peaceful retreats and lively locales. In the op-posite direction, west of Sivatha St, there are some friendly, family-run guesthouses.

NH6 has an incredible array of hotels, but it's a busy road and not the most charming part of town. Lacking the tranquillity of the river and far from the pulse of life, it doesn't offer much beyond discounted midrange hotels. Better is the road to Angkor, which has some of the best-known top-end hotels in town and, tucked away near the river, some of the best boutique hideaways.

Check out the **Siem Reap Angkor Hotel & Guesthouse Association** (www.angkor hotels.org) for a complete listing of guesthouses and hotels.

BEST FOR ROMANTICS
> Hanumanalaya (www.hanumanalaya .com)
> River Garden (www.therivergarden .info)
> Pavillon Indochine (www.pavillon indochine.com)

BEST VALUE
> Green Village Palace (www.green villagepalace.com)
> Shadow of Angkor (www.shadow ofangkor.com)
> Steung Siem Reap Hotel (www .steungsiemreaphotel.com)

BEST FOR OPULENCE
> Amansara (www.amanresorts .com)
> Grand Hotel d'Angkor (http://siem reap.raffles.com)
> La Résidence d'Angkor (www .residencedangkor.com)

BEST FOR COOL
> Golden Banana (www.golden-banana .com)
> Golden Temple Villa (www.golden templevilla.com)
> Hotel de la Paix (www.hoteldelapaix angkor.com)

TEMPLE VIEWS

So immense in size and scale is Angkor that it is one of the few ancient structures visible from space. Most people haven't got the US$20 million it takes to be a cosmonaut, so must go in search of their own atmosphere around Angkor. Whether you are seeking personal enlightenment for a brief moment in time or an inspired image to immortalise the experience forever, seek out some of these spectacular views.

Angkor Wat is the mother of all temples and has some views to die for. Standing by the ponds watching a sunrise is superb, but it's equally rewarding to sit in the eastern gateway and watch the sun reveal the central tower. The views from the upper level are immense and help put the size and scale into perspective. It's also possible to stare down over Angkor Wat from Phnom Bakheng, a hot-air balloon or a helicopter (see p133).

The gates of Angkor Thom almost floor you with their impact. The south gate is the most spectacular, but the view is often shared with tour buses and tourists galore. The east gate is the place for a serene view. Bayon is a jumble from afar, but during the magic hour just after sunrise, the light can pick out the faces to bring it to life. The real reward comes from venturing inside and viewing the enigmatic faces from every angle.

Other views that should not be missed include the tree roots of Ta Prohm at dawn; approaching the mighty Preah Khan from the east in late afternoon; looking out over the jungles of Cambodia from the Kbal Spean viewpoint; and seeing the pink sandstone of Banteay Srei begin to shimmer in the softer sunlight of late afternoon.

The days of serene and spiritual moments within the confines of empty temples are over: Angkor is on the tourist trail. However, with a little planning it is still possible to escape the hordes. Remember though that places are popular for a reason and it is worth going with the flow at least once.

The most popular place for sunrise is Angkor Wat. Most tour groups head back to town for breakfast, so stick around and explore the temple while it's cool and quiet. Bayon sees far fewer visitors than Angkor Wat in the early hours. Sra Srang is usually pretty quiet, and can be spectacular thanks to reflections in the extensive waters. Ta Prohm is an alternative option, with no sight of sunrise, but a mysterious and magical atmosphere.

The definitive sunset spot is the temple of Phnom Bakheng, but almost every visitor rocks up here. It's better to check it out for sunrise or in the early morning and miss the crowds. Pre Rup is popular for an authentic rural sunset over the rice fields, but it's starting to get crowded too.

When it comes to the most popular temples, the middle of the day is the quietest time, as the large groups head back to town for lunch, but it's also the hottest. If you pull up outside and see a car park full of tour buses, you may want to move on to somewhere quieter. The wonderful thing about Angkor is that there is always another temple to explore.

BEST FOR SUNRISE OR SUNSET
> Angkor Wat (p60)
> Bayon (p69)
> Phnom Bakheng (p77)
> Pre Rup (p87)
> Sra Srang (p79)

BEST OF THE REST
> Banteay Samré (p88)
> Preah Neak Poan (p85)
> Preah Khan (p83)
> Ta Keo (p82)
> Ta Som (p86)

BEST FOR JUNGLE
> Beng Mealea (p99)
> Kbal Spean (p101)
> Koh Ker (p102)
> Preah Palilay (p75)
> Ta Prohm (p79)

BEST FOR FILM BUFFS
> Angkor Wat (p60)
> Bayon (p69)
> Beng Mealea (p99)
> East Gate of Angkor Thom (p68)
> Ta Prohm (p79)

Top left Bakong Temple (p97) — one of the stunning monuments of Roluos

CARVINGS & RELIEFS

It could well be argued that Angkor is the world's largest open-air art gallery, with the walls of hundreds of temples adorned with thousands of exquisite carvings and reliefs. The ancient Cambodians may have been influenced by India in the early years, but before long they had defined a uniquely Khmer style that is one of the high-water marks of ancient artistry.

The bas-reliefs around Angkor (see picture below) are a veritable feast of Hindu myths and legends. Wrapping themselves around the base of famous temples such as Angkor Wat and Bayon, they are the jewels that make these crowning monuments sparkle. The detail is impeccable, with individual facial expressions, original clothing and many different animals featured; but the scale is superhuman, as these carvings are in perfect proportion, surreally symmetrical, and run for hundreds of metres. The ancient artisans wielded their chisels like a magician handles his wand.

No less impressive than the lengthy bas-reliefs at the principal temples are the incredible carvings covering the smaller structures. Pediments, lintels, doorframes, support beams – almost everything was turned into a piece of art by the ancient Khmers. Beautiful *apsaras* (heavenly nymphs) and *devadas* (goddesses) demurely guard the doors, giant *nagas* (serpents) uncoil themselves along the causeways, and the majestic heads of the Bodhisattva Avalokiteshvara survey the scene. There is simply so much beauty that it almost overwhelms

BEST CARVINGS

> 'Churning' bas-relief at Angkor Wat (p66)
> Bas-reliefs at Bayon (p71)
> Brick carvings at Prasat Kravan (p78)
> Pediments at Banteay Srei (p98)
> Riverbed carvings at Kbal Spean (p101)

BEST-KNOWN CHARACTERS

> *apsara* – heavenly nymph
> *essai* – Hindu wise man or ascetic
> *kala* – the temple guardian above doorways
> *makara* – giant sea serpent
> *naga* – multiheaded serpent on causeways and roofs

FOOD

It's no secret that the dining tables of Thailand and Vietnam are home to some of the finest food in the world, so it should come as no surprise to discover that Cambodian cuisine is rather special. Just as Angkor has put Cambodia on the tourist map, so too *amoc* (baked fish with coconut, lemongrass and chilli in banana leaf) could put the country on the culinary map of the world.

Cambodia has a great variety of dishes, some similar to the cuisine of neighbouring Thailand and Laos, others closer to Chinese and Vietnamese cooking. But all come with a unique Cambodian twist, be it the odd herb here or the odd spice there. The overall impression is that Khmer cooking has the aromas of India, the textures of Thailand and the subtlety of Vietnam.

Freshwater fish forms a huge part of the Cambodian diet thanks to the natural phenomenon of Tonlé Sap lake. They come in every shape and size, from the giant Mekong catfish to tiny whitebait (great beer snacks when deep-fried). The French left their mark too: baguettes are the national bread and Cambodian cooks show a healthy reverence for tender meats.

Rice and *prahoc* – a fermented fish paste that your nose will soon recognise at a hundred paces – form the backbone of Khmer cuisine. Cambodian meals almost always include *samlor* (soup). *Samlor machou banle* is a popular hot-and-sour fish soup with pineapple and a splash of spices.

BEST FOR ROMANTICS
> Abacus (p35)
> Le Malraux (p39)
> Les Orientalistes (p40)
> L'Oasi Italiana (p55)
> Madame Butterfly (p55)

BEST KHMER FLAVOURS
> Amok (p36)
> Angkor Palm (p36)
> Khmer Kitchen Restaurant (p38)
> Psar Chaa Stalls (p40)
> Sugar Palm (p41)

v

PUBS & CLUBS

Siem Reap was a late developer in terms of nightlife, but it's also a fast learner and has emerged to become one of the liveliest towns in the Mekong region. While the party towns of Bangkok and Saigon are winding down as police enforce closing times, Siem Reap is strutting its stuff, free of government meddling. You don't have to fight for your right to party here; it's rockin' every night and the revelry goes on from dusk 'til dawn.

Bar St (see picture below) is a dirty dozen of bars and pubs crammed into a short stretch of central Siem Reap. It's loud and proud, but it can get overwhelming with all the competing DJs. Warm up or wind down here, but only hit the midnight hour if you're looking for company.

Beyond Bar St are more individual places, with a definitive character and, sometimes, customer. There are Brit-style pubs with Sunday roasts and quiz nights, uberchic lounge bars with guest DJs and classy cocktails, plus the classic Cambodian plastic-chair-and-strip-light setup, lined with bottles of Angkor or ABC stout.

When it comes to clubs, Siem Reap is definitely not keeping up with Bangkok. There is a small scene that involves heavy techno hedonists dancing around their bottles of Chivas Regal or whichever spirit earns the most kudos that week. There are also some raunchier places promoting pole dancers, where karaoke definitely doesn't mean 'orchestra without voice' and the massage is sure to involve a 'happy ending'. Stick to the bars!

BEST LATE-NIGHT SPOTS
> Angkor What? (p42)
> Laundry Bar (p43)
> Temple Club (p43)
> Warehouse (p44)
> X Bar (p44)

BEST COCKTAILS
> Aha (p35)
> Arts Lounge (p42)
> Joe-to-Go (p42)
> Funky Munky (p42)
> Linga Bar (p43)

SHOPPING AROUND

It's a far cry from Bangkok, but despite the rough edges Siem Reap offers some smooth shopping opportunities. As well as the inevitable range of souvenirs, there are many high-quality handicrafts made to support disadvantaged groups in Cambodia. Markets are the cheapest option for shopping, but they can be claustrophobic and clammy. Shops are more refined and the prices more defined. The night market offers the best of both worlds, with stacks of stalls and cooler temperatures after dark.

Before venturing forth, learn a little about the art of bargaining. There are no fixed prices at market stalls and temple vendors, so there is room for negotiation. Make a lower counteroffer, engage in some friendly banter, and walk away if the price is not right. Remember that the aim is not to get the lowest possible price, but a price that is acceptable to both parties.

Cambodia is famous for its exquisite silk, much of which is still traditionally hand-woven. There are many skilled stone carvers and popular keepsakes include busts of Jayavarman VII and statues of Hindu deities. Don't attempt to buy ancient stone sculpture in Cambodia, as looting is a major problem. Other popular purchases include Cambodian silver, renowned for its intricacy, and woodcarvings of Hindu gods and Buddhas.

Don't forget to save some spending for the temples, as many of the villagers sell handicrafts, books, T-shirts etc and need a piece of the action.

BEST SHOPS HELPING CAMBODIA
> Artisans d'Angkor (p30)
> Rajana (p34)
> Rehab Craft (p35)
> Senteurs d'Angkor (p35)
> Tabitha Cambodia (p35)

BEST FOR FASHION
> Angkor Night Market (p34)
> Eric Raisina Workshop (p53)
> Jasmine (p34)
> Les Chantiers Écoles Silk Farm (p50)
> Samatoa (p35)

SPAS & MASSAGE

Reflecting Siem Reap's newfound status as an international destination, there are some super-swish spas (see picture below) and enough massage styles to rival the dining options. Try Chinese acupuncture, Japanese shiatsu, traditional Swedish, tough Thai, or Vietnamese suction-cup massage.

Some masseurs are stronger than others, and some techniques more persecution than pleasure, so only request a strong massage if you were a wrestler in an earlier life. Some of the more vigorous manoeuvres include a judo-style throw of the body to each side, and kneeling on your back while pulling the torso upwards. Ouch! But many of these are medicinal and you know what they say – no pain, no gain.

Foot-massage shops are spread around Psar Chaa and offer a range of remedies for dispirited soles. This is also the spot for some of the best spas in town, pampering palaces offering mud baths, herbal saunas, floral plunges and seaweed wraps. There are also massages by the blind to help empower the visually impaired community in Cambodia.

Siem Reap is littered with massage shops, but some offer more 'services' than others. Gentlemen should not be surprised to be offered a 'happy ending' in certain establishments, but the amount of make-up caking the face of the masseuse is usually a good indication that traditional massage may not be high on the agenda. That said, there is no real trick to selecting an authentic place, as we have heard stories of patrons at the smartest hotels being offered all sort of high jinks.

BEST MASSAGE
> Bodia Spa (p32)
> Bodytune (p32)
> Dr Feet (p33)
> Frangipani (p33)
> Seeing Hands Massage 4 (p33)

Offerings at Bantea Srei (p98)

BACKGROUND
HISTORY
THE GOLDEN AGE OF ANGKOR

The Angkorian period spans more than 600 years from AD 802 to 1432. During this time, the Khmer empire was to have a profound impact on mainland Southeast Asia, acting as a distillery for culture, religion and language from the Indian subcontinent. Like the Romans, the Khmers came, they saw, they conquered. They dominated this region for centuries, both suppressing and civilising their neighbours and leaving an indelible mark in the form of temples and highways, many of which remain today. Successive empires claimed the old Khmer cities as their own. If Europe owes a debt of gratitude to the Romans, Southeast Asia must thank the Khmers.

A popular place of pilgrimage for Khmers today, the sacred mountain of Phnom Kulen, to the northeast of Angkor, is home to an inscription that tells of Jayavarman II proclaiming himself a *devaraja* (god-king), the earthly representative of Hindu god Shiva, in 802. Jayavarman II then set out to bring the country under his control through alliances and conquests, and was the first monarch to rule most of what we call Cambodia today.

The key to the meteoric rise of Angkor was a mastery of water and an elaborate hydraulic system that allowed the ancient Khmers to tame the elements. The first records of the massive irrigation works that supported the population of Angkor date from the reign of Indravarman I (r 877–889), who built the *baray* (reservoir) of Indratataka. His son Yasovarman I (r 889–910) moved the capital to the Angkor area with the construction of the temple-mountain of Phnom Bakheng.

DEDICATION TO THEIR TEMPLES

The god-kings of Angkor were enthusiastic builders. Each king was expected to dedicate a temple to his patron god, most commonly Shiva or Vishnu during the time of Angkor. Then there were the ancestors, including mother, father and grandparents (both maternal and paternal), which meant another half-dozen temples or more. Finally there was the mausoleum or king's temple, intended to deify the monarch and project his power. All of these had to be bigger and better than one's predecessor's. This accounts for the staggering architectural productivity of the Khmers and the epic evolution of temple architecture.

Suryavarman II (r 1112–1152) extended Khmer influence to Malaya and Burma (Myanmar), but he also waged costly wars against Vietnam and Champa (now southern and central Vietnam). He is immortalised as the king who, in his devotion to the Hindu deity Vishnu, commissioned the majestic temple of Angkor Wat.

Suryavarman II had brought Champa to heel and reduced it to vassal status, but the Chams struck back in 1177 with a naval expedition into Tonlé Sap lake. They took the Khmers by surprise and executed King Dharanindravarman II. The following year a cousin of Suryavarman II rallied the Khmer troops and defeated the Chams. The new leader was crowned Jayavarman VII in 1181, and went on to become Cambodia's most celebrated king (see The Enigma of Jayavarman VII, p14).

DECLINE & ABANDONMENT

Angkor was the epicentre of an incredible empire that held sway over much of the Mekong region, but, as with all empires, the sun was to eventually set. By the turn of the 13th century, the irrigation network was already choking, slowly silting up due to the massive deforestation that had taken place in the heavily populated areas around Angkor. Massive construction projects such as Angkor Wat and Angkor Thom no doubt put an enormous strain on the royal coffers and on the people who subsidised them with hard labour and taxes.

Another challenge for the later kings was religious conflict. The state religion changed back and forth several times during the twilight years of the empire, and kings spent more time engaged in iconoclasm, defacing the temples of their predecessors, than building monuments to their own achievements. From time to time this boiled over into civil war.

Angkor was losing control over the peripheries of its empire. At the same time, the Thais were ascendant, having migrated south from Yunnan to escape Kublai Khan and the Mongol hordes. The Thais, first from Sukothai and later Ayuthaya, grew in strength and made repeated incursions into Angkor, finally sacking the city in 1431 and making off with thousands of intellectuals, artisans and dancers from the royal court. During this period, perhaps drawn by the opportunities for sea trade with China and fearful of the increasingly bellicose Thais, the Khmer elite began to migrate away from Angkor. The Khmer court moved to Phnom Penh and Angkor was abandoned to pilgrims, holy men and the elements.

> **RESERVOIR GODS**
> The *baray* (reservoir) was the first stage of an irrigation system that created a hydraulic city, the ancient Khmers mastering the cycle of nature to water their lands. It also had religious significance as, according to legend, Mt Meru is flanked by lakes. As is often the case, form and function work together in harmony.

EUROPEAN DISCOVERY

French naturalist and 'accidental tourist' Henri Mouhot is credited with the discovery of Angkor in 1860. But 'discovery', with all the romance it implies, is something of a misnomer. Portuguese explorers had visited in the 16th century, and even in 1860 Angkor Wat included a wealthy monastery. Mouhot made no such claims of discovery, as he died of malaria in Luang Prabang in 1861, but it was his account, with its rich descriptions and tantalising sketches of the temples, that turned the ruins into an international obsession.

The French annexed Cambodia as a protectorate in 1864 and began a long love affair with the temples of Angkor, researching the history and restoring the site. After independence from France in 1953, Cambodia enjoyed a period of peace and prosperity that saw Angkor emerge as the most popular tourist destination in Southeast Asia.

WAR & REVOLUTION

The good times were not to last and Cambodia was plunged into a bloody civil war in 1970, a sideshow spillover from the conflict in Vietnam. Prince Sihanouk tried to steer a neutral course through the turbulent waters of the Cold War, but he ultimately paid the price for trying to play both sides. The country was divided into two, with the North Vietnamese communists and their Khmer Rouge allies controlling much of the countryside, and the Republican government of Lon Nol controlling most of the towns. The temples of Angkor fell to the communists in the summer of 1970. The front line of fighting was midway between Siem Reap and Angkor Wat, but archaeologists were allowed to cross back and forth between 1970 and 1973 to continue their work at the temples. After 1973 all restoration work at the temples was halted and didn't really begin in earnest again until the UN came to town in 1991.

On 17 April 1975 the Khmer Rouge marched into Phnom Penh and, under Pol Pot's direction, implemented one of the bloodiest revolutions the world has ever seen. It was 'Year Zero': money was abolished, cities abandoned and Cambodia transformed into a Maoist, peasant-dominated, agrarian cooperative.

During the next four years, hundreds of thousands of Cambodians, including the vast majority of the country's educated people, were relocated to the countryside, tortured to death or executed. Hundreds of thousands more died of mistreatment, malnutrition and disease. About two million Cambodians died between 1975 and 1979 as a direct result of the policies of the Khmer Rouge. In late 1978 the Vietnamese invaded and overthrew the Khmer Rouge, who fled westward to the jungles bordering Thailand.

The Khmer Rouge were hellbent on severing all links with the past and Cambodian culture was decimated during their rule, with pagodas turned into pigsties, artists and dancers executed, and religions banned. However, the temples of Angkor endured, a symbol of the nation for even the destructive zealots of the Khmer Rouge. Their survival through such terrible times may yet offer Cambodia a brighter future.

ARCHAEOLOGY

Many of Angkor's secrets remain to be discovered, as most of the work at the temples has concentrated on restoration efforts above the ground rather than archaeological surveys below. Underground is where the real story of Angkor and its people lies – the inscriptions on the temples give us only a partial picture of the gods to whom each structure was dedicated and the kings who built them.

In 1901 the **École Française d'Extrême-Orient** (EFEO; French School of Asian Studies; www.efeo.fr) began a long association with Angkor with an expedition to Bayon. Initial attempts to clear Angkor were fraught with technical diffi-culties and theoretical disputes. On the technical front, the jungle tended to grow back as soon as it was cleared; on the theoretical front, scholars debated the extent to which the temples should be restored.

It was not until the late 1920s that a solution came along – anastylosis. This was the method the Dutch had used to restore Borobudur in Java. Put simply, it was a way of reconstructing monuments using the original materials and in keeping with the original form of the structure.

The first major restoration job was carried out on Banteay Srei in 1930. It was deemed such a success that many more extensive restoration projects were undertaken elsewhere around Angkor, culminating in the massive Angkor Wat restoration in the 1960s.

Most of Angkor's great temples were abandoned to the jungle for many centuries. At some monuments, such as Ta Prohm, the jungle had stealthily waged an all-out invasion, and plantlife could only be removed at great risk to the structures it now supported in its web of roots. This gives certain temples an air of abandonment and adds to the aura of discovery for the visitor.

The years of Khmer Rouge control and civil war in Cambodia resulted in a long interruption of restoration work, allowing the jungle to resume its assault on the monuments. The illegal trade of *objets d'art* on the world art market has also been a major threat to Angkor, although it is the more remote sites that have been targeted recently. Angkor has been a Unesco World Heritage Site since 1992 and was removed from Unesco's endangered list in 2003.

ARCHITECTURE

From the time of the earliest Angkorian monuments at Roluos, Khmer architecture was continually evolving. Archaeologists divide the monuments of Angkor into nine separate periods, named after the foremost temple of each period's architectural style.

The evolution of Khmer architecture was based around a central theme of the temple-mountain, preferably set on a real hill, but artificial if there weren't any mountains to hand. The earlier a temple was constructed, the closer it adheres to this fundamental idea. Essentially, the mountain was represented by a tower mounted on a tiered base. At the summit was the central sanctuary, usually with an open door to the east and three false doors.

By the time of the Bakheng period, this layout was being embellished. The summit of the central tower was crowned with five 'peaks': four at the points of the compass and one in the centre. Even Angkor Wat features this layout, though on a grandiose scale. Other features that came to be favoured included an entry tower and a causeway lined with *naga* (mythical serpent) balustrades leading up to the temple.

These refinements and additions culminated in Angkor Wat, which effectively showcases the evolution of Angkorian architecture. The architecture of the Bayon period breaks with tradition in temples such as Ta Prohm and Preah Khan, in which the horizontal layout of galleries, corridors and courtyards completely eclipses the central tower.

The curious narrowness of the corridors and doorways in these structures is explained by the fact that Angkorian architects never mastered the flying buttress to build a full arch. They engineered arches by laying blocks on top of each other, until they met at a central point; known as false arches, they can support only very short spans.

RELIGION

Ask most Cambodians about their religious beliefs and they'll say they're Buddhist. However, Cambodian Buddhism is an evolving and accommodating faith that has absorbed both Hindu and Animist beliefs from an earlier era. So intertwined are these faiths that it is hard to unravel them.

Hinduism and Buddhism co-existed from the 1st century AD until the 14th century. During the time of Angkor, Shiva was the deity most in favour with the royal family, although in the 12th century he was superseded by Vishnu. Today some elements of Hinduism are still incorporated into important ceremonies involving birth, marriage and death.

Buddhism came to Cambodia with Hinduism, but only became the official religion from the 13th or 14th century. Most Khmers today practice Theravada Buddhism. Between 1975 and 1979 the majority of Cambodia's Buddhist monks were murdered by the Khmer Rouge and nearly all of the country's wats (more than 3000) were damaged or destroyed. In the late 1980s, Buddhism once again became the state religion and today young monks are a common sight around Angkor.

Every Buddhist male is expected to become a monk for a short period in his life. Men or boys under 20 years of age may enter the Sangha (Buddhist community) as novices. Nowadays men may spend as little as 15 days to accrue merit as monks.

LIFE AS A SIEM REAP RESIDENT

Life for most residents in Siem Reap is a dizzying ride, as the town undergoes a metamorphosis from an overgrown village to a centre for the international jet set. The pace of change is electric and the young generation is embracing the new realities with enthusiastic abandonment, learning English, French, Japanese, Korean – anything that will give them a head start in this brave new world.

For many countryside Cambodians who live around Siem Reap, life is centred on family, faith and food, a timeless existence that has stayed the same for centuries. Family is more than the nuclear family we now know in the West; it's the extended family of third cousins and obscure aunts: as long as there is a bloodline there is a bond. Families stick together, solve problems collectively, listen to the wisdom of the elders and pool resources.

During the dark decades of the 1970s and 1980s, this routine was ripped apart by war and ideology, as peasants were dragged from all they held dear and forced into slavery. The Khmer Rouge took over as the moral and social beacon in the lives of the people, and families were forced apart, children turned against parents, brother against sister. The bond of trust was broken and is only slowly being rebuilt today.

Faith is another rock in the lives of many older Cambodians, and Buddhism has helped them to rebuild their lives after the Khmer Rouge. Most Siem Reap houses contain a small shrine to pray for luck, and the wats throng with the faithful come Buddhist Day.

Food is more important to older Cambodians than to most, as they have tasted what it is like to be without. Famine stalked the country in the late 1970s, and even today malnutrition and food shortages are common during times of drought.

But for the younger generation brought up in a postconflict, postcommunist period of relative freedom, it's a different story – arguably thanks to their steady diet of MTV and steamy soaps. Like other parts of Asia before it, Cambodia is experiencing its very own '60s swing, as the younger generation stands up for a different lifestyle than the one their parents had to swallow. This is creating plenty of friction in Siem Reap, as rebellious teens dress as they like, date who they want and hit the town until all hours. But few actually live on their own: they still come home to mum and dad at the end of the day and the arguments start again.

Young or old, Khmers love a good laugh, so make sure you pack your sense of humour. The children selling at the temples won't just pester you; they will engage in endless banter and have a one-liner for every occasion.

GOVERNMENT & POLITICS

Cambodia is at a crossroads on its road to recovery from the brutal years of Khmer Rouge rule. Compare Cambodia today with the dark abyss into which it plunged in the 1970s and it's a positive picture, but look to its more successful neighbours and it's easy to be pessimistic. Peace has come to the country, the economy is taking off and international organisations have helped to build a thriving civil society, but opportunities favour the few with close connections to the ruling party and the law is unevenly applied to suit the country's powerbrokers. Cambodia must choose its path: pluralism, progress and prosperity; or intimidation, impunity and injustice. The jury is still very much out on which way things will go.

Another jury still out is that of the Khmer Rouge trial, sidelined by the politics of the Cold War for two decades, and then delayed by bureaucratic bickering at home and abroad. The trial is finally underway, but it is by no means certain that the wheels of justice will turn fast enough to keep up with the rapid ageing of the surviving Khmer Rouge leaders. Keep up to date with the latest developments at www.cambodiatribunal monitor.org.

The royal family has been a constant in contemporary Cambodian history and no-one more so than the mercurial monarch King Sihanouk, who once again surprised the world with his abdication in 2004. His relatively unknown son King Sihamoni assumed the throne and is untainted by the partisan politics of the past.

But there's a new royal family in town, the ruling Cambodian People's Party (CPP), and they are making plans for the future with dynastic alliances between their offspring. At the head of this elite is Prime Minister Hun Sen, who has been in power for more than 20 years. Using his legendary chess skills to good effect in politics, he has checkmated rivals on more than one occasion.

Elections will be held again 2008, and it's predicted that the CPP will triumph again, with the opposition Sam Rainsy Party surging ahead, leaving the royalist Funcinpec party trailing a distant third.

POLITICS & PROFIT AMONG THE TEMPLES

Angkor Conservation is a Ministry of Culture compound on the banks of the Siem Reap River. It houses more than 5000 statues, *lingas* (phallic symbols) and inscribed steles, stored here to protect them from the wanton looting that has blighted hundreds of sites around Angkor. The finest statuary is hidden away inside Angkor Conservation's warehouses, meticulously numbered and catalogued. Unfortunately, without the right contacts, trying to get a peek at the statues is a lost cause. Some of the statuary is now on public display in the Angkor National Museum (p30), but it is only a fraction of the collection. In a further development, the Thai consortium behind the new museum now has control over Angkor Conservation.

Formerly housed at Angkor Conservation, but now going it alone in offices throughout Siem Reap, is Apsara Authority. This organisation is responsible for the research, protection and conservation of cultural heritage around Angkor, as well as urban planning in Siem Reap and tourism development in the region. Quite a mandate, quite a challenge – especially now that the government is taking such a keen interest in its work. Angkor is a money-spinner; it remains to be seen whether Apsara will be empowered to put preservation before profits.

Entry tickets to the temples of Angkor are controlled by local hotel chain Sokha Hotels, which in return for administrating the site takes the first US$3 million and 17% of the additional revenue per annum. Apsara Authority receives 10%, and the lion's share is returned to the Finance Ministry.

ECONOMY

Badly traumatised by decades of conflict, Cambodia's economy was long a gecko amid the neighbouring dragons. However, it's all changing, as investors are circling to take advantage of the new opportunities. Cambodia's economy is now among the fastest-growing in the world, hitting the magic 10%-a-year figure recently. It's a far cry from the days of civil war, genocide and famine.

Tourism is a very big deal in Cambodia, with more than two million visitors arriving in 2007, a doubling of numbers in just three years. In Angkor, Cambodia has something with which none of its more developed neighbours can compete. Thousands of tourism jobs are being created every year and this is proving a great way to integrate the huge numbers of young people into the economy. Wages are low by regional standards, but tips can add up to a princely sum that might support an extended family in some far-flung province.

Other important industries include the garment sector, where Cambodia is trying to carve a niche as an ethical producer, and rubber plantations, which are bouncing back after years of neglect. Oil and gas have been discovered off the coast of Cambodia and could be a major industry in years to come.

Foreign aid was long the mainstay of the Cambodian economy, supporting half the government's budget, and NGOs have done much to force important socio-political issues onto the agenda. However, with multibillion-dollar investments stacking up, it looks like the government may no longer be influenced by their lobbying.

Corruption remains a way of life in Cambodia. It is a major element of the Cambodian economy and exists to some extent at all levels of government. Sometimes it is overt, but increasingly it is covert, with private companies often securing favourable business deals on the basis of their connections. It seems everything is for sale in the new Cambodia – ancient temples, national parks and even the Killing Fields have been privatised.

ENVIRONMENT

Angkor was designated a national park in 1925, the first in Southeast Asia, and its protected status has ensured it remains a pristine environment even today. Where other great temple cities such as Ayuthaya in Thailand or Bagan in Burma (Myanmar) are surrounded by towns or hemmed in by hotels, Angkor remains isolated amid its protected forests. However, there are worrying signs for the future as visitor numbers soar into the millions. A trickle of barefoot pilgrims has given way to a tide of tourists in trekking shoes, and sandstone is notoriously soft. With so many temples to protect, looting has also been a huge problem: hundreds, if not thousands, of beautiful sculptures have been hacked off by art thieves and smuggled out of the region via Bangkok. The main temples of Angkor are now well protected and under the world's gaze thanks to their status as a World Heritage Site, but remote temples remain under threat.

Tourism is also creating environmental pressures of another kind, with hundreds of new hotels putting pressure on the area's water table. The government will need to improve water management and irrigation if tourism and agriculture are to co-exist. There is also no central waste-water management system and waste disposal is the responsibility of individual businesses, issues which some proprietors take more seriously than others. It is by no means a crisis, but action will need to be taken sooner rather than later, before the size and scale of the problems are beyond control.

BACKGROUND

FURTHER READING

When it comes to travelogues, the classic Cambodian read is Norman Lewis' *A Dragon Apparent: Travels in Cambodia, Laos and Vietnam* (1951), an account of his 1950 foray into an Indochina that would soon disappear. Henri Mouhot's *Travels in Siam, Cambodia, Laos and Annam* (1864) offers the inside story of the man credited with rediscovering Angkor.

Angkor has also starred in fiction. *The King's Last Song* (2006) by Geoff Ryman weaves together the story of Jayavarman VII with a contemporary drama involving kidnapping and the Khmer Rouge.

The Khmer Rouge turned the clocks to Year Zero in what was to become one of the world's most radical and bloody revolutions. The best-known of the survivor stories is *First they Killed My Father* (2001) by Luong Ung. *The Gate* (2003) by Francois Bizot tells of his kidnapping by the Khmer Rouge. He was the only foreigner to be released by Comrade Duch, later head of the notorious Tuol Sleng Prison.

TOP 10 BOOKS ON ANGKOR

> *A Guide to the Angkor Monuments* (Maurice Glaize) – the definitive guide to Angkor; download for free at www.theangkorguide.com
> *A Passage Through Angkor* (Mark Standen) – one of the best photographic records of the temples of Angkor
> *A Pilgrimage to Angkor* (Pierre Loti) – one of the most beautifully written books on Angkor, based on the author's 1910 journey
> *Ancient Angkor* (Claudes Jacques) – written by one of the foremost scholars on Angkor, this is the most readable guide to the temples
> *Angkor: An Introduction to the Temples* (Dawn Rooney) – probably the most popular contemporary guide available
> *Angkor – Heart of an Asian Empire* (Bruno Dagens) – the story of the rediscovery of Angkor, complete with lavish illustrations
> *Angkor: Millennium of Glory* (ed Helen Jessup) – a fascinating introduction to the history, culture, sculpture and religion of the Angkor period
> *Angkor: Splendours of the Khmer Civilisation* (Marilia Albanese) – beautifully photographed guide to the major temples, including some of the more remote sites
> *Khmer Heritage in the Old Siamese Provinces of Cambodia* (Etienne Aymonier) – Aymonier journeyed through Cambodia in 1901 and visited many of the major temples
> *The Customs of Cambodia* (Chou Ta-Kuan) – the only eyewitness account of Angkor, from a Chinese emissary who lived at Angkor in the late 13th century

A standout among the journo accounts is Jon Swain's *River of Time* (1995), which includes a first-hand account of the French embassy stand-off in the first days of the Khmer Rouge takeover. Tim Page's *Derailed in Uncle Ho's Victory Garden* (1995) covers this legendary photographer's quest for the truth behind the disappearance of photojournalist Sean Flynn (son of Errol) in Cambodia.

Among the historical accounts, *History of Cambodia* (1994) by David Chandler is the best all-rounder. *Pol Pot: The History of a Nightmare* (2004) by Philip Short is a detailed account of the Khmer Rouge leader's life, while *Prince of Light, Prince of Darkness* (1994) by Milton Osbourne examines the story of Sihanouk, a constant presence in the politics of modern Cambodia. *Sideshow: Kissinger, Nixon and the Destruction of Cambodia* (1979) by William Shawcross is a superb account of how Cambodia was sucked into the American war in Vietnam.

FILMS

The first major international feature film to be shot in Cambodia was *Lord Jim* (1964). This was credited with kick-starting Sihanouk's film career, which saw him direct, produce and star in many movies as Cambodia teetered towards the abyss.

Cambodia is once again attracting international film-makers. First came an Angkor cameo at the end of *In the Mood for Love* (2000), directed by Wong Kar-wai. It was quickly followed by Hollywood heavyweight *Lara Croft: Tomb Raider* (2001), which featured several temples around Angkor (see On Location with Tomb Raider, p71). Other big flicks include Jean-Jacques Annaud's *Two Brothers* (2004), with some stunning sequences shot around Angkor with tigers and elephants, and Matt Dillon's *City of Ghosts* (2002), shot all over Cambodia but resisting the lure of the temples.

The definitive film about Cambodia is *The Killing Fields* (1985), which tells the story of American journalist Sydney Schanberg and his Cambodian assistant Dith Pran. Schanberg was evacuated from the French embassy, leaving Pran to face the horrors of Khmer Rouge rule.

Cambodian director Rithy Panh's *People of the Rice Fields* was nominated for the Palme d'Or at the Cannes Film Festival in 1995. *S-21: The Khmer Rouge Killing Machine* (2003) is his powerful documentary in which survivors from Tuol Sleng Prison are brought back to confront their guards.

DIRECTORY
TRANSPORT
ARRIVAL & DEPARTURE

Arriving by air is straightforward these days, with a smart new international airport and visas available on arrival. Entering Cambodia by land is still something of a challenge, thanks to overcharging for visas, transport scams and rollercoaster roads, but it's a real adventure.

AIR

All international flights arrive at the **Siem Reap International Airport** (REP; Map p59; ☎ 063-380283; www.cambodia-airports.com/siemreap/en), gateway to the temples of Angkor. There are no direct flights between Cambodia and the West, so all visitors will end up transiting through an Asian hub such as Bangkok, Hong Kong or Singapore.

The airport has a good range of services, including restaurants, bars, shops and ATMs, and there are few hassles. Arrange a taxi into the town centre, 7km away, for US$5. Motorbike taxis are also available for just US$2. If you have already booked accommodation in Siem Reap, the rate may include a free transfer.

BOAT

Siem Reap is located a short distance from the vast Tonlé Sap lake and visitors can connect to Battambang or Phnom Penh by fast boat. Whichever fast-boat journey takes your fancy, you may well end up on the roof, so make sure you use sun block and wear a head covering.

The boats between Siem Reap and Phnom Penh (US$20 to US$25, five hours or more, 7am departure daily) are horrendously overcrowded and foreigners are charged twice the price of Khmers for the 'privilege' of sitting on the

CLIMATE CHANGE & TRAVEL

Travel, especially air travel, is a significant contributor to global climate change. At Lonely Planet we believe that all who travel have a responsibility to limit their personal impact. As a result, we have teamed up with Rough Guides and other concerned industry partners to support Climate Care, which allows people to offset the greenhouse gases they are responsible for with contributions to energy-saving projects and other climate-friendly initiatives in the developing world. Lonely Planet offsets all staff and author travel.

For more information, turn to the responsible travel pages on www.lonelyplanet.com. For details on offsetting your carbon emissions and a carbon calculator, go to www.climatecare.org.

roof. It is not the most interesting boat journey in Cambodia, as Tonlé Sap lake is like a vast sea, offering little scenery.

The small boat between Siem Reap and Battambang (US$15, three to eight hours depending on the season, 7am departure daily) is more rewarding, as the river scenery is truly memorable, but it can take forever.

Boats from Siem Reap leave from the floating village of Chong Kneas near Phnom Krom, 11km south of Siem Reap. The boats dock in different places at different times of the year; when the lake recedes in the dry season, both the port and floating village move with it.

Boat tickets bought from guesthouses usually include a *moto* (motorcycle taxi) or minibus ride to the port. Otherwise, a *moto* out here costs about US$2, a *remorque-moto* (tuk tuk) about US$4 and a taxi around US$10.

LAND

Siem Reap is plugged into the Cambodian road network and offers connections to the Thai border and Bangkok beyond. NH6 connects Siem Reap to the Cambodian capital of Phnom Penh and buses (from US$5, 317km, six hours) make the run daily. A rugby scrum of *moto* and *remorque-moto* drivers awaits incoming buses

and it can get physical. It is also possible to travel by private car or share taxi.

To the west, Siem Reap is connected to the Thai border at Poipet and buses (US$10, 148km, three to four hours) run daily. It is also possible to travel by private car, share taxi or pick-up truck.

The land borders with Thailand are open from 7am to 8pm daily. Be aware that some Cambodian immigration officers at the crossings have a reputation for overcharging for the visa in Thai baht (anywhere between 1000B and 1200B instead of 700B), or forcing tourists to change US dollars into riel at a poor rate. Hold your breath, stand your ground, but don't start a fight. There are now international ATMs in Poipet.

Coming from Bangkok, there are two slow trains a day from Hualamphong train station to Aranya Prathet (48B, six hours) near the Cambodian border. There are also regular bus services from Bangkok's Mo Chit northern terminal to Aranya Prathet (1st/2nd class 200/160B, four to five hours). From Aranya Prathet, take a tuk tuk for the final 6km to the border for about 80B.

Avoid the touts when crossing into Cambodia and don't listen to any offers of help in securing a visa. Stay solo and walk to the bus company offices for sensible fares. It is also possible to negotiate a taxi if you can avoid the taxi mafia; try to pay no more than US$40 to Siem Reap. Otherwise climb aboard a pick-up truck to Sisophon (50B), where there are onward connections to Siem Reap.

TRAVEL DOCUMENTS

Travellers visiting Cambodia need to ensure their passport is valid for at least six months beyond the date of arrival. Also ensure you have at least one free page for the visa.

VISA

Most visitors to Cambodia require a one-month tourist visa (US$20), available on arrival at Siem Reap International Airport and nearby land borders. One passport-sized photo is required. It is also possible to arrange a visa through Cambodian embassies overseas or an online e-Visa (US$25) through the **Ministry of Foreign Affairs** (http://evisa.mfaic.gov.kh), which helps prevent overcharging at some land crossings.

DEPARTURE TAX

There is a departure tax of US$25 on all international flights out of Siem Reap International Airport. The airport tax for domestic flights to Phnom Penh is US$6.

GETTING AROUND

Central Siem Reap is pretty easy to navigate on foot, as it is quite a compact town at heart. However, visitors staying further out of town will need to use local transport from time to time, such as *motos*, *remorque-motos* or private cars.

When it comes to the mighty temples of Angkor, it is important to consider the most suitable way to explore. Tourists on organised trips are likely to travel around the area by coach, minibus or car, but for the independent traveller there is a tempting range of alternatives to consider. The weather may dictate the choice to some extent, as during the wet season it is best to opt for some protection from the rain.

For the ultimate Angkor experience, try a pick-and-mix approach, with a *moto, remorque-moto* or car for one day to cover the remote sites, a bicycle to experience the central temples, and an exploration on foot for a spot of peace and serenity.

For more remote temples such as Banteay Srei or Beng Mealea, prices are higher than those suggested here, due to extra fuel costs.

BICYCLE

A great way to get around the temples, bicycles (US$2 per day) are environmentally friendly and

ALTERNATIVE FORMS OF TRANSPORT

For an unconventional approach to Angkor, try a bird's-eye view from a helicopter or hot-air balloon or a leisurely lollop on an elephant.

Elephant

Travelling by elephant was the traditional way to see the temples way back in the early days of tourism at Angkor. It is once again possible to take an elephant ride between the south gate of Angkor Thom and the Bayon (US$10) in the morning, or up to the summit of Phnom Bakheng for sunset (US$15). The elephants are owned by the **Angkor Village** (www .angkorvillage.com/elephants.php) group and are well looked after.

Helicopter

For those with plenty of pocket money, there are tourist flights around Angkor Wat (US$75) and the temples around Angkor Thom (US$130) with **Helicopters Cambodia** (Map p29, C4; ☎ 012 814500; www.helicopterscambodia.com; 658 Hup Quan St). The company also offers charters to remote temples such as Koh Ker and Prasat Preah Vihear, with prices starting at around US$1800 per hour. Newcomer **Sokha Helicopters** (Map p29; ☎ 017 848891; www .sokhahelicopters.com; Sivatha St) offers cheaper sightseeing flights.

Hot-Air Balloon

The **Angkor Balloon** (Map p59; ☎ 012 844049; flights US$15) operates on a fixed line and rises 200m above the landscape, offering pretty impressive views over Angkor Wat. It's located about 1km west of Angkor Wat on the road towards the airport.

are used by most locals living around the area. There are few hills and the roads are good, so there's no need for much cycling experience.

The **White Bicycles** (www.thewhite bicycles.org) initiative is worth supporting, as proceeds from the US$2 hire fee go towards community projects. Several guesthouses around town promote the project. Electric bicycles (US$4) are available for hire, but make sure the battery is fully charged before setting off.

BOAT

It's not possible to visit the temples via their moats just yet, but there are several opportunities for boat trips in the Siem Reap area. Cruises through the floating villages of Tonlé Sap lake are the main draw, but it is also possible to visit Prek Toal Bird Sanctuary or the ruined Western Mebon temple in the Western Baray.

CAR & 4WD

Cars are a popular choice for getting about the temples. The drawback is that visitors are a little more isolated from the sights, sounds and smells. A car with driver around the central temples costs US$25 to US$30 per day and can be arranged with hotels, guesthouses and agencies in town.

A 4WD isn't necessary for the vast majority of Angkor's temples, but it can be a more comfortable option for remote sites such as Koh Ker. Think US$80 and up per day.

MOTO

Some independent travellers visit the temples by motorcycle taxi. *Moto* drivers accost visitors from the moment they set foot in Siem Reap, but they often end up being knowledgeable and friendly. Most drivers charge about US$8 per day. *Moto* drivers also whisk people about town by day or night. Motorcycle rental is currently prohibited in Siem Reap.

REMORQUE-MOTO

Often called a tuk tuk, this is a motorcycle with a twee little hooded carriage in tow. They are a popular way to get around Angkor as fellow travellers can talk to each other as they explore, and they offer some protection from the rain. Like *moto* drivers, some *remorque* drivers are very good companions for a tour of the temples. Prices range from US$10 to US$20 per day, depending on the destination and number of passengers. *Remorques* are also available as 'taxis' around town.

PRACTICALITIES
BUSINESS HOURS

Cambodians rise early and it is not unusual to see people exercising at 5.30am if you are heading home – ahem, sorry, getting up – at that time. Government offices are supposedly open from 7.30am to 5pm, with a break for a lunchtime siesta. However, few people will be around early or after 4pm, as their main income is earned elsewhere.

Banking hours vary, but core hours are 8.30am to 3.30pm

NEGOTIATING A FAIR FARE

Many visitors to Siem Reap use local transport to get around the town, particularly at night. Whether you choose a *moto* or *remorque-moto*, it is best to negotiate the fare in advance. For short distances, *moto* fares should be up to 2000r; *remorques* about US$1. Later at night this may well double; prices also rise if you are heading to a hotel further out of town. If you are staying at a superswish hotel, be aware that drivers may round the price up considerably. The more people you stuff in a *remorque*, the more the price goes up.

Monday to Friday, plus Saturday morning. Tourist attractions such as the temples and local museums are normally open seven days a week, including lunchtime.

Local restaurants are generally open from about 6am until 9pm; international restaurants open late morning (some open for breakfast too) and close around 11pm. Some bars are open all day, but others open only for the night shift, especially if they don't serve food.

Local markets operate seven days a week and usually open and close with the sun, running from 6.30am to 5.30pm. Shops tend to open from about 7am until 8pm, sometimes later.

ELECTRICITY

The usual voltage is 220V, 50 cycles, but power surges and cuts are common, particularly beyond the city centre. Electrical sockets are usually two-holed, and accept flat or round pins. Bigger hotels have multipin sockets, and adaptors are available cheaply.

EMERGENCIES

Siem Reap is one of the safest places in Cambodia, so there is no real need to worry about personal safety. However, bag snatching is common in the capital Phnom Penh and it can only be a matter of time before thieves try their luck in Siem Reap. The **tourist police** (☎ 012 969991) are based at the main ticket checkpoint for the Angkor area.

Ambulance (☎ 119)
Fire service (☎ 118)
Police (☎ 117)

In case of any serious medical problems, it is best to head to Bangkok. However, there are a couple of good places in Siem Reap:

Angkor Children's Hospital (Map p29, C3; ☎ 063-963409; www.angkorhospital.org; Samdech Tep Vong St; 24hr) A paediatric hospital of international standard, this is the place to take children if they fall sick.

Royal Angkor International Hospital (☎ 063-761888; www.royalangkorhospital .com; Airport Rd; 24hr) A new international facility, affiliated with the Bangkok Hospital.

U-Care Pharmacy (Map p29, B2; ☎ 063-965396; Pithnou St; 8am-9pm) Smart pharmacy with English spoken.

HOLIDAYS

It's official: Cambodia has more public holidays than any other nation on earth. The following is just a selection; there are also holidays for Khmer New Year in mid-April and Chinese New Year some time in January or February.

International New Year's Day 1 January
Victory Over the Genocide 7 January
International Women's Day 8 March
International Workers' Day 1 May
International Children's Day 8 May
King's Birthday 13–15 May

King Mother's Birthday 18 June
Constitution Day 24 September
King Father's Birthday 31 October
Independence Day 9 November
International Human Rights Day
10 December

INTERNET

It is hard to walk the streets of Siem Reap without stumbling upon an internet café, and access is cheap at US$0.50 per hour. Wi-fi access is available at several cafés and restaurants, plus some midrange to top-end hotels.

Check out some of these websites when planning your trip:
Andy Brouwer's Cambodia Tales (www .andybrouwer.co.uk) A great gateway to all things Cambodian, this site includes travel articles from veteran Cambodian adventurers.
ChildSafe (www.childsafe-cambodia.org) Learn about the ChildSafe campaign, which aims to stop child sex tourism and is raising awareness of the problem.
Heritage Watch (www.heritagewatch.org) The home of the heritage-friendly tourism campaign to raise interest in remote heritage sites and their protection.
Stay Another Day (www.stay-another-day .org) A great website dedicated to tempting tourists into staying another day in Siem Reap, packed with ideas on day trips, project visits and alternative sights.
Tales of Asia (www.talesofasia.com) Up-to-the-minute information on overland travel in Cambodia, including the infamous Bangkok–Siem Reap run.
Yellow Pages (www.yp.com.kh) The place to track down that phone number that has changed yet again.

LANGUAGE

The Khmer language is nontonal, which may be a relief for those who have struggled with Thai or Vietnamese. Learning a few key phrases will earn instant friends, as Cambodians love to see visitors making an effort. While spoken Khmer may be easier than some languages, the script is harder, as it is derived from Sanskrit and Pali and includes 33 consonants and 24 vowels and diphthongs.

BASICS

Hello.
  johm riab sua/sua s'dei
Goodbye.
  lia suhn hao-y
Hi. How are you?
  niak sohk sabaay te?
I'm fine.
  kh'nyohm sohk sabaay
Excuse me/I'm sorry.
  sohm toh
Yes.
  baat (used by men)
  jaa (used by women)
No.   *te*
Please.   *sohm*
Thank you.   *aw kohn*
You're welcome.
  awt ei te/sohm anjœ-in
Does anyone here speak English?
  tii nih mian niak jeh phiasaa awngle te?
I don't understand.
  kh'nyohm muhn yuhl te/ kh'nyohm s'dap muhn baan te

How much is it?
nih th'lay pohnmaan?
That's too much.
th'lay pek

EATING & DRINKING

This is delicious.
nih ch'ngain nah
I'm a vegetarian.
kh'nyohm tawm sait
Please bring the bill.
sohm kuht lui

EMERGENCIES

I'm sick.
kh'nyohm cheu
Help!
juay kh'nyohm phawng!
Call a doctor!
juay hav kruu paet mao!
Call the police!
juay hav polih mao!

DAYS & NUMBERS

today	*th'ngay nih*
tomorrow	*th'ngay s'aik*
yesterday	*m'suhl mein*

1	*muy*
2	*pii*
3	*bei*
4	*buan*
5	*bram*
6	*bram muy*
7	*bram pii/puhl*
8	*bram bei*
9	*bram buan*
10	*dawp*
11	*dawp muy*

19	*dawp bram buan*
20	*m'phei*
21	*m'phei muy*
30	*saamsuhp*
40	*saisuhpw*
50	*haasuhp*
60	*soksuhp*
70	*chetsuhp*
80	*paedsuhp*
90	*cowsuhp*
100	*muy roy*
1000	*muy poan*

MONEY

COSTS

Siem Reap covers the whole spectrum. Budget travellers with an eye on enjoyment can live it up on US$25 per day. Midrange travellers can turn on the style with US$75 to US$100 a day, staying in smart places, dining well and travelling in comfort. At the top end, flash US$200 or more and you can live a life of luxury.

CURRENCY

Cambodia's currency is the riel, abbreviated in this guide to a lower-case 'r' written after the sum. Cambodia's second currency (some would say its first) is the US dollar, which is accepted everywhere and by everyone, though change may arrive in riel. Dollar bills with a small tear are unlikely to be accepted in Cambodia. The Thai baht (B) is also sometimes used in Siem Reap. If three currencies seems excessive, don't forget the Cambodians are making up for lost time: during the Pol Pot era, the country had *no* currency. The Khmer Rouge abolished money and blew up the National Bank building in Phnom Penh.

The riel comes in notes of the following denominations: 50r, 100r, 200r, 500r, 1000r, 2000r, 5000r, 10,000r, 20,000r, 50,000r and 100,000r.

Throughout this book, prices are in the currency quoted to the average punter, whether in US dollars or riel. For a sprinkling of exchange rates at the time of going to print, see the Quick Reference in the inside front cover of this book.

ATMS

There are ATMs all over Siem Reap these days, with ANZ Royal the best represented. Cash comes in US dollars and the limit is often up to US$2000 if your home account can handle it. Many banks levy a small charge.

CREDIT CARDS

Top-end hotels, airline offices, smart restaurants and upmarket boutiques generally accept most major credit cards (Visa, Master-Card, JCB, sometimes American Express), but they usually pass the charges straight on to the customer, meaning an extra 3% on the bill.

Cash advances on credit cards are available for those who are experiencing uncooperative ATMs. Canadia Bank and Union Commercial Bank offer free cash advances.

EXCHANGING MONEY

Armed with enough US dollars, you won't need to visit a bank – it is possible to change small amounts of dollars for riel at hotels, restaurants and markets. It's always handy to have about US$10 worth of riel kicking around, as it is good for *motos* and markets.

TRAVELLERS CHEQUES

It is easiest to have cheques in US dollars, though it's also possible to change euros and most major currencies at the bigger banks. There is usually a 2% commission to change travellers cheques.

NEWSPAPERS & MAGAZINES

The *Cambodia Daily* is a popular English-language newspaper, while the *Phnom Penh Post* offers in-depth analysis every two weeks. For up-to-date information on Siem Reap, pick up a copy of the *Siem Reap Angkor Visitors Guide* (www.canbypublications.com), which is packed with listings and comes out quarterly. For further insights into the restaurant and bar scene in Siem Reap, see the

Siem Reap Drinking & Dining guide, produced by Pocket Guide (www .cambodiapocketguide.com), the team behind the *Siem Reap Out & About* guide to spas and shopping.

ORGANISED TOURS

Armed with this guide, Angkor is pretty easy to navigate on your own, but there are quite a few experienced operators than can add something special to your encounter. The following companies are recommended as they offer something a little different from the ordinary, such as remote temples, hidden villages or ecotourism initiatives.

About Asia (☎ 092 121059; www.asia travel-cambodia.com) Small bespoke travel company specialising in Siem Reap. Profits go to building schools in Cambodia.

Buffalo Trails (☎ 012 297506; buffalotrails @online.com.kh) Promotes homestays, bird-watching, traditional fishing techniques and Cambodian cooking classes.

Hanuman Tourism (☎ 023-218396; www .hanumantourism.com) Long-running local company with innovative tours like Temple Safari. Operates the Hanuman Foundation.

Journeys Within (☎ 063-964748; www .journeys-within.com) Operates a small boutique hotel in Siem Reap and has a charitable arm, Journeys Within Our Community (www .journeyswithinourcommunity.org), helping schools and communities.

La Villa (☎ 092 256691; www.thevilla siemreap.com) Small group trips to more remote spots like Beng Mealea temple and Kompong Phhluk village.

Paneman (☎ 063-761759; www.paneman .org) Ecotourism company that operates bio-diesel boats on Tonlé Sap lake and arranges specialist trips around Angkor.

Sam Veasna Centre (☎ 063-761597; www.samveasna.org) Established ecotourism operator specialising in bird-watching tours around Siem Reap and Cambodia. Supports conservation and education.

Terre Cambodge (☎ 063-964391; www .terrecambodge.com) Offers trips to a variety of remote sites around Angkor, plus boat trips on Tonlé Sap lake by wooden sampan.

PHOTOGRAPHY & VIDEO

Most internet cafés in Siem Reap will burn CDs or DVDs from digital images using card readers or USB connections. Digital memory sticks are widely available in town and are pretty cheap. Print film costs around US$2.50 and processing works out at about US$4 for a roll.

If you carry a video camera, make sure you have the necessary charger, plugs and transformer for Cambodia. Take care with some of the electrical wiring in guesthouses, as it can be pretty amateurish. If you are shooting on hi-def, pick up tapes before arriving in Siem Reap.

TELEPHONE

If you are travelling with a mobile phone on international roaming, just select a network upon arrival, dial away and await a hefty phone bill once you return home. Note to self: Cambodian roaming charges

DIRECTORY

are extraordinarily high. Cambodia operates on the GSM 900/1800 bands, compatible with most parts of the world except the US. Americans travelling with quad-band phones should have no problems.

Local calls are usually pretty cheap, even from hotel rooms. Calling from province to province is considerably more expensive by fixed lines. The easiest way to call is to head to one of the many small private booths on the kerbside, with prices around 300r per minute.

The cheapest way to call internationally is via internet phone. Most shops and cafés that provide internet services also offer internet calls. Calls usually cost between 200r and 2000r per minute, depending on the destination. Most internet cafés also provide webcams, so you can see family and friends while catching up on the gossip. However, lines aren't always that clear if traffic is high, so consider the handy tourist SIM card. This costs US$10 and can be inserted in any unlocked mobile phone. Calls are cheap at just US$0.25 per minute, but the card lasts for only 10 days from activation. Cards are available at hotels, shops and stalls around town.

COUNTRY & CITY CODES

All numbers in this guide are listed with area codes, but you can drop the initial 063 if calling from within Siem Reap. Mobile numbers begin with 01 or 09; in these cases you do need to dial all the numbers, even when calling locally.

Cambodia	☎ 855
Phnom Penh	☎ 023
Siem Reap	☎ 063
Sihanoukville	☎ 034

USEFUL PHONE NUMBERS
International direct dial code
☎ 001 or 007

....

TIPPING

Tipping is not traditionally expected here, but in a country as poor as Cambodia, tips go a long way. Salaries remain extremely low and service is often superb. A tip of just US$1 might be half a day's wages for some. Many of the upmarket hotels levy a 10% service charge, but this doesn't always make it to the staff. Don't forget to tip the staff who clean your room. Consider tipping drivers and guides, as time on the road means time away from home and family.

It is considered proper to make a small donation at the end of a visit to a wat, especially if a monk has shown you around; most wats have contribution boxes for this purpose.

....

TOURIST INFORMATION

Tourist information offices are almost nonexistent in Cambodia. The best sources of up-to-date information are the free guides distributed around Siem Reap, recommended under Newspapers & Magazines (p138).

Cambodia has no official tourist offices abroad, and Cambodian embassies aren't really much help in planning a trip, apart from issuing visas.

TRAVELLERS WITH DISABILITIES

The biggest challenge in Cambodia also happens to be the main attraction: the temples of Angkor. Causeways are uneven, obstacles common and staircases daunting, even for able-bodied people.

On the positive side, Cambodian people are usually very helpful towards all foreigners, and local labour is cheap. Most guesthouses and small hotels have ground-floor rooms that are reasonably easy to access.

There is now a growing network of information sources that can put you in touch with others who have conquered Angkor before. Try the following:

Gimp on the Go (www.gimponthego.com)
Mobility International USA (www.miusa.org)
Society for Accessible Travel & Hospitality (SATH; www.sath.org)

>INDEX

See also separate subindexes for See (p145), Do (p145), Shop (p145), Eat (p145), Drink (p146) and Play (p146).

000 map pages